St. John's Hospital Training School

The Nursing sister

A manual for candidates and novices of hospital communities

St. John's Hospital Training School

The Nursing sister
A manual for candidates and novices of hospital communities

ISBN/EAN: 9783337173647

Printed in Europe, USA, Canada, Australia, Japan

Cover: Foto ©Lupo / pixelio.de

More available books at **www.hansebooks.com**

THE NURSING SISTER

A MANUAL

—FOR—

CANDIDATES AND NOVICES

—OF—

HOSPITAL COMMUNITIES.

PREPARED BY

St. John's Hospital Training School

SPRINGFIELD, ILLINOIS.

1899.

SPRINGFIELD, ILL.;
H. W. Rokker Co., Printers and Binders.
1899.

Entered according to Act of Congress, in the year 1899, by
REV. L. HINSSEN,
In the office of the Librarian of Congress.

PREFACE

In compiling this manual, several hand-books of nursing have been consulted and their contents more or less used. My motive for adding another to the many useful and excellent books on nursing already in existence was, because I have not succeeded so far in finding a single one among them exactly adapted to meet the special wants of young beginners in Hospital communities, viz.: the candidates and novices. Most of them as a rule apply for admission to the community when they are yet very young. All are actuated by the holiest motives which religion inspires, to devote their lives to the alleviation of suffering humanity for Christ's sake, but are often without much experience of practical life and with no knowledge of Hospital work whatever. Many a candidate loses her courage before the first year of probation is at an end on account of the great task before her, viz.: of learning within the two years of probation the prescribed hand-books and all practical work that is required of a nurse if she expects to pass the last examination successfully. Undoubtedly, the practical side of the training of a nurse is the most important one, but the theoretical instruction must go hand in hand with it. The latter, as a rule, offers the most difficulties for young beginners. Many of the inevitable difficulties might be lessened if the best method of meeting them is pursued. After some years of practical experience in our Training School this best method seemed to be, to analyze at the daily instructions the particular chapter on the art of nursing, in short, well chosen questions and answers, easy to remember, and then let the practical instruction follow. This is the history of the origin of the present Manual. It is a short, popular guide on the art of nursing, which gives the substance of larger hand-books, and prepares the candidates and novices gradually and easily for the study of more difficult books on nursing and the final examination. The method has been tried in our Training School and has proved a complete success.

L. H.

CONTENTS.

Chapter I.
Qualifications of the Nursing Sister, Personal Appearance, Her Conduct Toward the Doctor, the Patient, the Family and Servants, Meals, Rest and Exercise. ... 1–14

Chapter II.
The Sick Room, Private Room in Hospital, Hospital Wards ... 14–20

Chapter III.
Deodorizer, Thermometer, Ventilation, etc. ... 20–24

Chapter IV.
Changing and Airing of Bed Clothes, etc. ... 24–29

Chapter V.
Bathing ... 29–31

Chapter VI.
Bed Sores, Giving Medicine ... 32–34

Chapter VII.
Things Important to Write Down, Clinical Record ... 34–36

Chapter VIII.
Food at Night, Manner of Serving Meals, etc. ... 37–41

Chapter IX.
Observation of Symptoms ... 41–48

Chapter X.
Bed Making, Laying Out Corpse ... 48–52

Chapter XI.
Cleaning of Room, Washing, Bathing Patient, Changing of Clothes ... 52–54

Chapter XII.
Ventilation, Temperature, Taking of Temperature ... 54–57

CONTENTS.

CHAPTER XIII.
Bandaging 57-62

CHAPTER XIV.
Night Watching, Food, Medicine..................... 62-65

CHAPTER XV.
Atomizer, Bed Rest, Catheter......................... 65-68

CHAPTER XVI.
Enemas, Syringe, Bed Pans, etc...................... 68-81

CHAPTER XVII.
Leeches, Cupping, Poultices. 81-91

CHAPTER XVIII.
Counter Irritants..................................... 91-95

CHAPTER XIX.
Lotions, Liniments, Ointments........................ 95-97

CHAPTER XX.
Cold Applications.................................... 97-99

CHAPTER XXI.
Hot Applications, Dry Fomentations.................. 99-102

CHAPTER XXII.
Baths, Cold Douche, Hot Plunge Bath, Sponge Bath, Vapor Bath, Cold Plunge Bath...................102-111

CHAPTER XXIII.
Massage..112-113

CHAPTER XXIV.
Special Medical Cases, Typhoid Fever..............113-124

CHAPTER XXV.
Diet List for Convalescents of Typhoid Fever......124-126

CHAPTER XXVI.
Typhus, Scarlet Fever, Smallpox...................126-133

CHAPTER XXVII.
Chickenpox. Measles, Spasmodic Croup..............133-136

CONTENTS. VII

CHAPTER XXVIII.
Membraneous Croup..................................137–140
CHAPTER XXIX.
Diphtheritis, Whooping Cough........................141–144
CHAPTER XXX.
Pneumonia..144–148
CHAPTER XXXI.
Pleurisy, Cholera Morbus, Asiatic Cholera............148–152
CHAPTER XXXII.
Diarrhoea, Dysentery, Intestinal Colic, Hepatic Colic..152–154
CHAPTER XXXIII.
Gastritis, Dyspepsia, Peritonitis, Appendicitis.........154–158
CHAPTER XXXIV.
Sore Throat, Bronchitis, Asthma......................158–160
CHAPTER XXXV.
Laryngitis, Catarrh, Dropsy..........................160–162
CHAPTER XXXVI.
Bright's Disease, Renal Colic, Urticaris, Eczema......162–164
CHAPTER XXXVII.
Herpes, Itch, Cerebral Apoplexy, Paralysis............164–168
CHAPTER XXXVIII.
Neuralgia, Epilepsy, Hysteria, St. Vitus Dance........168–172
CHAPTER XXXIX.
Cerebral Meningitis, Rheumatism, Malaria Fever......172–176
CHAPTER XL.
Temperature, Pulse, Respiration, Urine...............176–183
CHAPTER LXI.
Disinfecting in Communicable Diseases................183–187
CHAPTER XLII.
Surgical Nursing, Wounds, Operations.................187–206

Chapter XLIII.
Laparotomy 206–210

Chapter XLIV.
Rules for Sisters in the Surgical Ward and Operating Room 210–211

Chapter XLV.
Gynaecological Cases 211–216

Chapter XLVI.
Fractures, Hemorrhage 217–226

Chapter XLVII.
Emergencies, Fractures and Dislocations 226–235

Chapter XLVIII.
The Human Body 235–252

I.

THE NURSING SISTER.

Q. What are the essential qualifications of a Sister of Charity?

1. Love of God and fellow-creature.
2. Good religious and secular education.
3. Purity of intention: all for Jesus.
4. Strength of body and mind.
5. Cheerful disposition.
6. Cleanliness to perfection.
7. Equanimity of mind.
8. Patience and perseverence.

Q. What else is required of a Sister that has to nurse the sick?

She must be well trained, conscientious and confidential.

Q. What is necessary in all cases of serious illness?

In all cases of serious illness, whether a Sister can be secured or not, there should be a certain person in the house who should be responsible for the patient to the physician.

Q. What will be the consequence if two or three persons take charge of a patient?

If two or three different persons take orders and report symptoms it will invariably cause confusion and mistakes; there must be but one head.

Q. What distresses a patient more in a Sister than in a stranger?

Want of order and common sense.

PROFESSIONAL NURSE.

Q. How will a well-trained and conscientious nurse deal with all her patients?

A really conscientious nurse will deal as kindly and faithfully with the poor and hospital patients as those sick in pleasant homes.

Q. When is a Sister generally called for private nursing outside the hospital?

A Sister is ordinarily called to a private family when the family is worn out and needs immediate relief.

Q. What can a Sister therefore not expect when she is called for private nursing?

A Sister can not expect to begin with a good night's rest, though she may arrive tired and after a long journey.

Q. How will the Sister generally find a family at her arrival?

Exhausted from care, watching and anxiety, and for this reason she must be ready to shoulder the burden which they are not able to bear a moment longer.

Q. What must she therefore do?

She must at once take her official position, not waiting to be told what to do, but commencing at once what is to be done.

Q. What should she realize?

She should realize that a life is entrusted to her keeping and that she alone is responsible to the physician.

Importance of Personal Appearance.

Q. What will much help towards inspiring the patient's confidence for a sister?

A pleasant personal appearance.

Q. How can this be secured?

It can be secured by extreme neatness in dress, clean handkerchiefs and aprons, attention to the skin, the hands, the teeth, etc. All these things distinguish a well trained sister from an ignorant one.

Q. What should be worn at night?

Warm night slippers.

Q. What should be avoided?

Bundling up in shawls, which are likely to catch in things and do mischief.

KEEPING HANDS IN ORDER.

Q. What should be done to keep the hands in order?

A few drops of glycerine rubbed in at night will keep the hands smooth if care is taken to wipe them dry each time they are put in water?

Q. What water is best used on hands?

Hot water is thought better than warm or cold.

Q. To what should a nurse accustom herself in using her hands?

To a light touch.

Q. For what reason?

A sensitive patient is often disturbed by the weight of a hand, or by moist, clammy hands.

ANOTHER AID TO MAKE A SISTER PERSONALLY ACCEPTABLE.

Q. What else will aid in making a Sister personally acceptable to the patient?

Great care in frequently changing and airing her clothes.

Q. What removes disagreeable odors from sweats, etc?

A few drops of ammonia in the water used for washing will remove disagreeable odors from perspiration.

Q. What will be very refreshing and can be accomplished easy?

A daily bath, with a simple basin and towel, in the following manner: Wring out a rough cloth in soap and water, and rub yourself briskly from head to foot.

Q. How long will this bath take?

Five minutes will suffice each day and help in keeping you healthy, fresh and pleasant.

Q. What should never be done in the presence of a patient?

Never trim your finger nails, though they must be kept scrupulously clean: never use an ear or tooth-pick.

Conduct Towards Servants.

Q. How should a sister conduct herself towards the servants of a family?

She should be careful not to cause them unnecessary trouble and work.

Q. What should she always acknowledge?

Any little service rendered, by saying, thank you.

Q. What should you let them feel?

Let them feel as far as possible, that you have come to share, not to increase the extra work, that sickness always brings to a house.

Q. What should the sister do with the dishes used for the patient?

The sister should wash and return to their places cups, plates, spoons, etc., used for the patient.

Q. To what should she not add unnecessary?

To the laundry.

Conduct Towards the Family.

Q. What has the family to expect from a sister?

The family has a right to expect from a sister a cheerful, helpful spirit in all things.

Q. About what should she not be too particular?

She should not be too particular about the dignity of her vocation.

Q. What is her duty towards the doctor?

To carry out all his orders.

Q. What must she do for the patient?

All that is essential for the patient in the way she knows best.

Q. After doing this, what should she be ready to accept from the family?

Besides this there are many little things, about which she should cheerfully accept the suggestions from members of the family, doing them in their way, to please them.

Q. What should the sister never forget?

She should never forget that the family have a burden of anxiety to bear, when a dear member is seriously ill.

Q. How should a sister try to lighten this burden?

She should try to lighten this burden by a kind and considerate manner towards all the household.

Q. What should the sister remember?

She should remember that she is responsible to the family as well as to the physician, whose orders she must follow.

About the Meals of the Sister.

Q. What understanding should she make about the meals?

For the patient's sake, as well as for her own, and in obedience to the rules of the community, the sister should request the family where she is nursing, from the beginning, that her meals be served alone out of the sickroom.

Q. What should a sister never betray towards a patient?

She should never betray towards a patient, by looks or words, any lack of consideration, and try to settle every thing peacefully and quietly.

Q. To Whom Does Her Time Belong?

The time of the sister belongs to those who have employed her.

Q. What can the sister do if she has some time at leisure?

If the patient is not seriously ill, there may be many hours, during which the sister can assist the family in sewing, after she has finished the needle work brought from the hospital.

Q. Where should the sister never bring her sewing?

The sister should, on no account, bring her sewing in the presence of any sick person or convalescent.

Q. What must the sister avoid besides this?

She must never turn up the gas bright in a sickroom in order to be able to sew or knit.

Q. Why?

Because the bright light is not pleasant to the eyes of a sick person. Moreover one gas burner consumes a large amount of air needed for the patient.

REST AND EXERCISE.

Q. When can a sister take rest, when her patient is very ill?

If the patient is very ill, rest can only be taken at odd times, when he can safely be trusted with some member of the family.

Q. What is very important for the sister to cultivate in regard to sleep?

She should accustom herself to the habit of light sleep.

Q. What is often necessary with very ill patients?

It some times is necessary to be wide awake all night.

Q. What should a sister provide for in this case?

In this case the sister must not neglect to provide for a cup of coffee and some refreshments, to be taken if possible, in an adjoining room.

Q. What else should be kept in an adjoining room?

The little things and utensils necessary to use in care of the sick.

Q. What must a sister be allowed occasionally?

She must be relieved occasionally from her work, and allowed at least four hours undisturbed sleep, and a little exercise in the fresh air not less than twice a week.

Q. In what case does the sister get sufficient fresh air?

In cases where she is permitted to go to mass in the morning.

Q. If there is no arrangements made for this what should the sister do?

The sister should pleasantly ask for relief.

Q. In case relief is not given, is she allowed to show dissatisfaction?

Never. Nor should she show unwillingness to go to the patient, even when off duty, and never let him see that she is tired or disturbed about anything.

BEFORE ENTERING THE ROOM.

Q. What should be done before entering the patient's room?

The mantle should be taken off.

Q. What next?

Make herself ready for work, inform herself where towels and clean linen are kept, where to put soiled clothing, and where to empty and wash vessels.

HOW TO GREET A PATIENT.

Q. How can you best greet a patient on seeing him the first time?

On entering the room the first time, a pleasant look or bow are sufficient.

Q. What will make you acquainted with the patient?

The first service skillfully rendered will make you acquainted with the patient and often confirm or destroy his confidence in you.

Q. Where should the sister not sit in the sick room?

She should not sit, where the patient cannot help seeing her: she should not appear to watch him, though she must observe him constantly.

WHISPERING IN A SICK ROOM.

Q. What may whispering in a sick room be called under circumstances?

There may be circumstances in which a whispered conversation may be called cruelty against the patient.

Q. Why?

Because it is impossible that the patient's attention should not be strained to hear what is whispered.

Q. What is also injurious for the same reason?

Walking on tip toes and moving stealthily about the room.

Q. What will seldom annoy the patient?

A low, distinct tone, when conversation is necessary, and a light step will seldom annoy.

Q. Will a patient easily complain of things that annoy him?

No; a patient will often refrain from complaining of these things, lest he should be thought selfish.

Q. What must a sister do, therefore, in regard to these things?

She must all the more take care to protect the patient from them.

OTHER THINGS THAT DISTURB A PATIENT.

Q. What other things disturb a patient?

Sitting on the bed, the rattling of newspapers, the turning over of leaves with a snap, the swinging of a rocking chair, sewing, and the clicking of knitting needles, one or all, are sometimes seriously annoying to the patient.

Q. What injures a patient mostly?

Unnecessary or unexplained noise, though slight, injures a sick person much more than necessary noise of a much greater amount.

HOW TO PROMOTE THE PEACE OF MIND AND SERENITY OF THE PATIENT.

Q. How can a sister promote the peace of mind and serenity of her patient?

She can do this by moving about quietly, promptly putting things in their places knowing the right thing to do.

Q. How should she do all these things?

Without any hurry.

The Nursing Sister.

Q. What should the sister never ask of the patient?

The sister should not call upon the patient to give his decision on anything, or let him be startled by anyone or anything.

Q. What should the sister always anticipate?

She should anticipate little wants, but never question in regard to them.

Q. What should the sister not do if the patient is delirious?

She should not contradict him.

Q. But what should she do in this case?

She should humor his notions quietly, whatever they may be, or say nothing unless questioned.

Q. What must be carefully avoided in fever delirium?

All appearance of fear.

Q. Where must the sister do her thinking?

She must do her thinking inside of her head, and not oblige the patient to hear her say, for example: "There! I must go and see about that beef tea, but I guess I'll wash up the spoons first," etc.

Q. How should a sister listen to the patient?

The sister should listen attentively to the patient when he speaks, and never ask him to repeat.

Q. Is it advisable for a sister to speak to the patient from a distance?

Never, from a distance, or standing behind him.

Q. How should she shut a door, and how can creaking be prevented?

Shut the door quickly and softly, oil the hinges, if rusty, to prevent squeaking.

OTHER THINGS THAT ARE NEVER TO BE SPOKEN OF BEFORE A PATIENT.

Q. About what may a sister never speak to a patient?

She may on no account speak of the sicknesses and diseases of other patients, or of disagreeable hospital experiences, operations performed, and sufferings witnessed, newspaper reports of crimes and calamities, or anything that may excite painful emotions.

Q. How should every conversation of the sister with the patient be?

It should be cheerful, brief, not too loud.

Q. From what should the sister divert the patient always?

She should divert the patient always from gloomy thoughts, and avoid too much talking of any kind.

The Symptoms of a Sick Person not a Topic of Conversation.

Q. Of what else should a sister never speak in the presence of the patient?

She should never speak of the symptoms unless questioned by the doctor.

Q. What more should the sister avoid?

Never give an unfavorable opinion of his condition to any one in his hearing.

Low Spirited Patients.

Q. What should a sister do with a low spirited patient?

If she can conscientiously encourage a patient, she should do so.

Q. How should she best do this?

Keep him cheerful and free from anxiety.

Q. What should the sister do on her part?

She should never look gloomy or anxious herself, or give up hope while there is life.

Insensible Patients.

Q. What should a sister never say in the presence of an insensible patient?

Though a patient seems insensible or in a stupor, never say anything loud in his presence which he ought not to hear.

Q. Why?

His hearing may be acute, though he may not be able to speak or move.

DUTIES TOWARDS THE DOCTOR.

Q. What duties has a sister towards the doctor?

She must implicitly obey all his directions, carefully report in writing every symptom and the exact history of the day since his last visit.

Q. What must she encourage on the patient's part?

She must encourage full confidence in the doctor on the part of the patient.

Q. What may a sister never discuss?

She may never discuss the doctor's treatment of the case.

A SISTER NOT JUSTIFIED IN LEAVING A CASE WITHOUT PERMISSION.

Q. Is a sister allowed to leave a case whenever she pleases?

Having once assumed the responsibility of a patient, it is her duty to remain with the patient as long as she can be of any use, unless obedience or her own health obliges her to leave.

Q. What should she do if the case has become chronic or incurable?

In this case the sister is not obliged to remain, but she should follow the directions of her superiors.

Q. How long is a sister allowed to remain out nursing without special permission?

One week at a time, except there is a probability that the patient will soon die.

SUGGESTIONS FOR A SISTER.

Q. What should a sister never speak of on her return from nursing?

Tales out of school.

Q. What may a sister never talk about?

Never about her own exploits in nursing, personal items of physician, or other things, out of the hospital, neither before the family, nor single patients, or in recreation.

Q. What ought a sister feel regarding all this?

She should remember, that gossip, though it may gratify curiosity for the moment, will not in the end increase the respect for the sister, nor for religious in general.

Q. How should a sister be in her mind and manners?

A sister should have in her thoughts, the purity of intention, and in her manners, be meek and firm, in her words, discreet and prudent.

Q. What must a sister preserve in all occurences of her vocation?

She must preserve purity of heart, the modesty of her eyes, and guard her tongue.

Concerning Callers.

Q. What will a sister, who respects herself, never allow whilst on duty?

No sister who respects herself will ever allow her duties to be interrupted or neglected by callers.

Q. In what points must a sister be extremely careful?

In the matter of so-called private friendships, for they are forbidden by the rule and dangerous to virtue.

Q. What are often the consequences of such friendships?

Every woman, and more so a religious, will injure her reputation for life, if she associates with unworthy persons, men or women, or with those to whom the slightest suspicion attaches.

Q. How should a sister associate with men?

Her conduct should be modest, earnest and brief, not more than what is necessary.

Q. When can a sister be a great comfort and aid in a family?

In times of greatest distress, or when it is clear that the patient is dying, then quiet self-possession and sincere sympathy will be of the first importance.

Q. What should a sister do in this case?

She should do all she can for the patient, and then, if not needed, stand aside, that the family may be nearest to him.

Q. When death has come, is there any need of hurry?

When death has come, there is no need, as in hospital wards, to hurry along the arrangements.

Q. How long should the relatives be left undisturbed.

Until they leave the room voluntarily.

Q. What may be done then, and how should it be done?

Then a sister may do what is necessary. She should be very careful that everything is done tenderly, and that great care is taken against exposure.

Q. What can the sister do after the corpse is laid out?

She should leave the room, clothing, etc., in perfect order, and put out of sight medicine or other traces of the sickness.

Q. What should be done with the bedclothes, etc.

All bedding, towels and clothing should be taken to the laundry; the windows in the room should be opened wide, the shutters closed.

SPECIAL OBLIGATIONS FOR A SISTER TO CONSIDER ALL CONFIDENTIAL COMMUNICATIONS OF THE PATIENT SACRED.

Q. What is a sister bound to hold sacred?

She is bound to hold sacred the confidences which she may have received from a patient, and never betray any family secrets, and her good reputation must follow her in this respect wherever she goes.

Q. What will be the consequence if a sister is not careful in talking about family affairs?

If it is once known that a sister likes to gossip, then she will bring disgrace upon the hospital where she comes from and the religious life in general.

Telling Sad News.

Q. What is the sister sometimes called upon to tell the patient?

It may sometimes happen that the sister is called upon to tell the patient that death is near.

Q. Without whose permission should this never be done?

Without the doctor's permission.

Q. In what case should she not do it at all?

If there be any member of the family, or clergyman, or other person to whom the duty rightfully belongs.

Q. If a sister must speak, how should she do it?

She should speak with the greatest possible gentleness.

Q. What is death to many a weary wanderer?

Death is a relief for many a weary wanderer on earth and it will be a consolation for him that he will soon be released through death from his sufferings. A sister must show all courage of a Christian soul, and tact of a wise nurse at the time of death of a patient.

Q. Without what qualities is a sister not fit for a nurse?

Without a quiet, cheerful Christian faith no woman is properly fitted for a nurse, especially not when a patient is dying.

The Patient's Room.

Q. What room is the best for a patient?

A room on the south side of the house which has an open fire-place.

Q. What should a sister do if such a room can be had?

Should there be such a room to which the patient can be removed, the sister should pleasantly suggest the change to the family.

Q. What should be done if the fire-place be stopped up?

If the chimney is stopped up with a fire-board, newspapers, blower or bunch of straw, the sister should at once remove it and make the chimney free.

The Nursing Sister.

Q. How should the room be kept?

Bright and cheerful, unless the condition of the patient requires it darkened.

Q. Should the sunlight be left in or not?

Let the sunlight in freely, always shading the patient's face.

Q. What should the sister do if the bed faces the window?

She should turn it around or, better, set up a screen.

Q. What is very trying on the eyes of a patient?

Bars and streaks from ill-fitting blinds are very trying on the eyes.

Q. Should the bed stand up close to the wall?

The bed should be pulled out from the wall as far as possible, that the air may have an access to it from all sides, and the sister may move easily about it.

Q. If the physician prefers a darkened room what should the sister do?

The sister must accustom herself to moving about quietly in it and let no consideration for her own convenience lead her to object to the order of the doctor.

Q. What should be carried out of the room?

All ornaments and anything not needed, for it will only make a lodging place for the dust.

Q. What should be done with rocking chairs?

Take away rocking chairs that visitors may not be tempted to swing in them.

Q. How should the washstand be kept?

Everything about the washstand should be kept clean.

Q. Where should the various little things be kept?

If there is no adjoining room or closet in which the various little matters which you require in your work may be put, then keep them out of sight behind a screen.

Private Rooms in a Hospital.

Q. How should the walls of a private room in a hospital be?

Either whitewashed or painted in a light color.

Q. What may hang on the walls?

Nothing but a crucifix.

Q. How shall the floor be?

The floor should be oiled, varnished or painted and a rug along side of the bed.

Q. What furniture?

A bedstead with springs (iron one preferred), mattress and bed-clothes, wardrobe, bureau, washstand, two chairs, easy chair, bedside, table and commode.

Q. What kind of goods may be used for cushions, tidies and covers?

Only washable goods.

Hospital Wards.

Q. What is absolutely necessary in a hospital ward?

The first requisite is scrupulous cleanliness.

Q. Why?

1. Because in a ward there are a greater number of lives at stake.

2. No amount of ventilation will keep the air fresh in a ward that is not clean.

Q. What is dust in a ward?

Not only dirt, but danger.

Q. Of what does dust consist?

It consists largely of organic matter, which must be taken away, not merely stirred up and redistributed.

Q. How can this be done?

By carefully dusting and sweeping the floor with a damp broom, with long strokes, and washing the floor frequently with clear water which cannot be changed too often.

Q. What is the consequence, if a ward is swept carelessly and clouds of dust are raised?

The dust will be driven over the beds and into the eyes and mouths of its unfortunate occupants, who cannot get out of the way, but can only stay and be choked, or their lungs affected by poisonous germs.

Q. What must be immediately removed from the wards?

All vessels must be immediately removed upon use, and thoroughly cleaned. Never bring a slop pale into the ward, all waste matters, even water used for washing, should be at once carried out.

Q. What should at once be removed besides this?

All soiled clothes. Before sending them to the laundry, see that there be no pins left in them, that they are distinctly marked with the letter of the ward, and if private property, with the number of the room or ward and name of the patient. Roll every dirty thing in a bundle by themselves.

Q. What takes the first and what takes the second place in a ward?

Cleanliness, everywhere next to Godliness, takes precedence in a hospital ward of all other virtues: Order, heaven's first law, has a secondary but still very important place. A well kept ward is characterized by neatness and uniformity.

Q. What adds a great deal to the attractive appearance of a ward?

A little care to have things straight. The beds should be in an exact line, chairs, tables and rugs at the same angle, to each other. No clothes may be tucked about the beds or flung over the chairs.

Q. What must be inspected daily?

The bedside tables, and no rubbish allowed to accumulate in them.

Q. What is often the consequence if this is neglected?

The patient will be apt to stow away dirty clothes, remains of meals, dead flowers, apple peels or any refuse that may need to be disposed of.

Q. What may never be thrown away.

Nothing that can in any way be utilized. If supplies are furnished liberally it should not be thought, those little bits are of no account, but they should be made to go as far as possible.

Q. Why?

Because hospital supplies are expensive and it is the sisters duty to see that nothing is wasted.

Q. What else must a sister do regarding these supplies?

She must see that they are well kept up, everything expected, to be on hand, renewed before quite exhausted and always kept in the same place, so if wanted they can easily be found.

Q. How can much confusion be avoided?

By getting every thing ready, even the smallest detail, before beginning the process. Have a clear idea in mind of what is to be done and never get excited. You will then be able to be prompt without hurrying, quite and methodical in movement, and will doubtless soon achieve a reputation as a neat and skillful nurse.

BEDSIDE TABLES.

Q. What should be placed for the patient's use at the head of the bed?

A small, light table, with a drawer.

Q. What should be placed on this table?

A glass of water or of cracked ice, covered with a saucer or a napkin.

Q. What else may be placed upon this table if the case permits?

An orange nicely prepared in little sections; just large enough for a mouthful, or any other ripe fruit, if the doctor permits.

Q. Upon what should the fruit be placed?

Over a bowl in which there is ice.

Q. Is there anything else that may be allowed to be placed upon this table?

A few very fresh flowers, nothing else.

Q. What should be done if there is a stationary wash stand in the room.

The Nursing Sister.

If there be a stationary wash basin in the room, put in the plug, and fill the basin full of water, which must be changed from time to time.

Q. What may be stuffed into the basin?

. A towel, and then cover it with a stiff paper or board.

Q. Should anything be emptied in this basin?

Never should anything be emptied into it, nor should the basin be used in any way.

Reasons for Not Using Stationary Washstands.

Q. Why should no water, used for any purpose in a sick room, be emptied into a stationary washstand?

The water you bath your patient in, or use for any purpose about the sick room, is very impure, and if emptied into the basin will form a slime round the pipes, and the impurity will escape into the room again in the form of foul air.

Q. How is often the waste pipe of a stationary basin?

It is almost sure to be defective, sooner or later, and sewer gas may rise through it from other parts of the house or from the streets and poison the air of the sick room.

Slop Pails.

Q. Should slop pails be allowed in a room?

Slop pails should never be allowed in a sick room.

Q. How should vessels be carried out?

All vessels should be carried out of the room, emptied and washed immediately, and towels kept constantly clean for this purpose.

Bedpans and Other Vessels.

Q. Where should bedpans and other urinals never be kept?

Never allow vessels, bedpans or urinals to stand, where they can be seen, either by patients or by persons coming into the room.

Q. Where should they be kept?

In a closet or adjoining room, if possible, and never put them under the bed.

Q. Where can they be placed for instant use?

If they must be ready for instant use, put them near the bed, and throw a clean towel over them.

Q. What should be kept in the vessels?

Always keep a deoderizer in them.

Q. What shall be put in the water in which they are washed?

Put a little washing soda or soap in the water.

Q. What should be done with vessels before bringing them to the patient?

Vessels should be warmed before they are brought to the patient, if the weather is cold.

A Deoderizer.

Q. What makes a splendid deoderizer?

A pound of sulphate of iron (copperas) dissolved in two quarts of rainwater, makes an excellent deoderizer, and has no disagreeable smell.

Q. How can it be used?

Pour a little into the vessels after washing them, and keep it in them.

Q. What effect has this on towels?

This mixture will stain towels.

A Disinfectant for Vessels.

Q. What will make a good disinfectant?

The following mixture: Water, two and one-half gallons; sulphate of iron, two pounds; carbolic acid, four pounds.

Q. How can it be used?

In communicable diseases, in typhoid fever and dysentary, always keep it in the veseels, and pour some in the closet every day.

Thermometer.

Q. How high should the thermometer in a sickroom be?

Never let the thermometer rise above 70 degrees, unless in special cases, such as croup, when the doctor's directions must be followed.

THE NURSING SISTER.

Q. How high should temperature be at night?

From 60 to 65 degrees, unless the doctor direct otherwise; ask him about it.

VENTILATION.

Q. Are cold rooms always well ventilated?

By no means; the air in a cold room may be very impure?

Q. What else can at times be suggested for good ventilation?

That a door be swung rapidly and quietly back and forth; it will force the bad air out of the room, and draw in the fresh air from the window, which is down at the top.

THE DOOR IN THE HALL.

Q. Why should the door of a sick room not be left open into the hall?

Because you cannot ventilate a room by merely having the door open into the hall. Only the stale air comes into the room, and the noise is heard from the whole house.

Q. In what case should the door into the adjoining room be left open?

If the adjoining room can be ventilated through an open window.

Q. For what time would this suffice?

This would be sufficient for night.

FUMIGATING.

Q. What is to be said about fumigating?

That the burning of pastilles, or coffee, the sprinkling of perfume, etc., does not purify the air; it simply covers the bad air.

Q. From where alone does clean air come?

Only from the outside of the house.

Q. How can you protect a patient while ventilating?

By placing a screen before the window or arranging the blinds or shutters so there be no direct draft on the patient.

Q. If there is an open fireplace in the room, what should be done?

Put a lighted lamp or candle in it.

Q. For what purpose?

This will draw the foul air up the chimney, while the fresh air from the window takes its place.

Q. What will do, if there cannot be a constant fire kept up in the fireplace.

A few sticks, lighted several times a day, and the lamp kept burning at all other times in the chimney, will secure constant ventilation.

Q. How often should the windows be opened wide in a sick room?

If the case permits, three times a day, at least.

Q. If this cannot be done, what can be done instead?

An adjoining room can be filled with fresh air, waiting until it is warmed a little, then opening the door and letting the fresh air into the sick room.

Q. In what case is the patient not allowed to breathe in the cold air?

In all cases that involve the throat, lungs or nasal passages, croup, sore throat, diphtheria, pneumonia, typhoid, scarlet fever and measles, which occasion to be throat troubles. In all these cases the patient must be covered and remain so until the fresh air be sufficiently warmed.

Putting the Room in Order.

Q. Whose duty is it to keep the patient's room in order and what does it require?

It is the sister's duty, and requires good management and common sense.

Q. What time should it be done?

Choose the time when the patient will be least disturbed, which is generally after breakfast.

Q. What must the sister avoid if she intends to put the room in order?

She must never move about restless, fussy, when the patient is eating.

Q. What should be used for dusting?

Never use a feather duster; dust the furniture, woodwork, etc., with a cloth.

Q. Where is the rug put and how is the carpet swept?

The rug should be hung in the air. Dip a cloth in water and wring it out dry and pass it quickly over the carpet.

Q. Where is this especially necessary?

Under the bed; for this purpose, therefore, the cloth can be fastened around the broom.

Q. What should be put around the bed while the moving is going on?

A screen.

Q. When can the room be cleaned thoroughly?

Only when the patient can be moved out for a while.

WHERE BOTTLES, SPOONS AND GLASSES BE KEPT.

Q. Where should glasses, spoons, etc., be kept.

All of these things should be kept out of sight on a table.

Q. What is to be done if the medicine is changed?

The boxes and bottles which are no longer needed should be set aside in a closet so as to avoid mistakes.

Q. How can you avoid the staining of spoons from the medicine?

By having a bowl of water with the medicine and keeping the spoons in it.

Q. What is mostly used for giving medicine?

A graduated glass.

Q. In what case must a spoon be used?

When the medicine is oily.

Q. What should always be on hand with the medicine?

One or two cloths to wipe the glass or spoon after it is washed.

Q. If you have a medicine glass for one person alone, how often should it be washed?

As often as it is used.

Q. Where should all washing of spoons and glasses be done?

Out of the patient's room.

Q. Why?

Because the rattling is very annoying for the patient.

How to Change the Bedclothes.

Q. How can you change the under sheets?

Fold the under sheet, then remove the soiled sheet with the same motion which puts on the fresh one.

Q. What must first be done with the sheet?

It must first be warmed and aired, then fold half of it up small and flat through its whole length, lay the folded part next and close to the patient, pushing before it the soiled under sheet folded in the same way.

Q. How can the sheets then be put under the patient?

Press down the mattress close by the patient and gently work the two folds, the soiled and the clean one, under the back. The head and the feet can be slightly raised to allow the folds to pass: after this is done you have only to pull the sheet smooth and tuck it in.

Q. What should be done with the pillows?

They should be changed several times a day; slip a cool fresh one under the patient's head and take away the warm one.

Q. If the bed is wide what can be done for the patient's comfort?

The patient can be gently moved from one side to the other, turning and never dragging him, and always have a fresh one ready for the night.

Q. How can the upper sheet be changed?

Air and warm the sheet and then roll it in its width; pass it under the sheet which you are to change, commencing at the foot of the bed and bring it up as smoothly as possible, unrolling it as you move it up.

Q. What shall be done with the soiled sheet when the clean one is over the patient?

It should be drawn down and removed at the foot end of the bed.

Q. What can be avoided in this way?

Removing the blankets and chilling the patient.

SECURING A FRESH FEELING BED WITH A FEW SHEETS.

Q. What ought to be changed often?

Sheets ought to be changed oftener than they commonly are.

Q. What is to be done if the supply is limited?

Then keep at least two upper sheets in use at one time, and alternate them, take the one that has been in use all day and hang it in another room to air.

Q. What sheet is to be put over the patient at night?

The sheet which has been hanging in another room to air since morning, but care must be taken that it is not damp or chilly.

Q. For what purpose?

This will help to secure a good night for the patient.

Q. What should be done with the patient as soon as he is well enough to be lifted?

He should then be lifted upon a lounge, then carry the mattress and pillows and bedding out of the room and air them by an open window.

Q. What is the best covering for a bed?

Clean sheets and blankets; no heavy quilt or counterpane should be used.

Bed for Long Occupation.

Q. With what must a bed be protected in case of serious illness?

With a rubber sheet and a draw-sheet, which must be large enough to be laid across the bed under the patient and be tucked in well at the sides.

Why is the draw-sheet used?

Because it can easily be removed and changed with very little disturbance to the patient, and is necessary also in order to protect him from the heating effect of the rubber cloth, which, if too near the person, promotes weakening perspiration.

Airing Clothing, Etc.

Q. Where should the airing of the clothing be done?

No clothing in use, no flannel or damp towels should be aired in the sick room. Soiled articles of all kinds should at once be removed.

Q. How many night-dresses should be kept in use?

Two: one for the day and one for the night. Always hang the one you take off by an open window for awhile, and warm it before using it again.

Q. How many sets of blankets should be kept in use?

Two, if possible; airing one set in the open air while the other is in use.

The Patient.

Q. How can you lift a very ill patient from one bed into another?

The bed should be made ready for use and pushed close to the one occupied. Two, or better, four persons, should then take by its corners the sheet upon which the patient lies, and very slowly and gently lift and place him on the fresh bed, removing the sheet after he has rested awhile.

Q. If there be only one sister to do this, how can she proceed?

Then the clean bed must be of the same height as the one occupied. A large rubber cloth should be laid under the patient, who is drawn with it to the edge of the bed.

Q. How far must the rubber cloth extend?

It must extend over the fresh bed and make a smooth surface, to cross which the patient can easily be pulled on a drawsheet to the fresh bed, and the rubber cloth may be removed.

Q. Should a patient help himself?

Never, if he is very ill. Never let him sit up or turn himself alone. Make it your rule to save his strength in every way.

LIFTING A HELPLESS PATIENT.

Q. What should be done if a patient has slipped down in bed?

He should then be put on his pillows again, but he must never be dragged.

Q. How can he be lifted upon the pillows?

If the patient is strong enough, he can clasp his hands around the neck of the sister, by this, distributing his weight more equally. The sister will generally find it easy to gently lift him up an inch from the bed and raise him upon the pillows.

Q. What should the sister do if the patient is too heavy?

If the patient is too heavy and too helpless to use his arms, it is better to drag the sheet upon which he is lying up towards the bed head, and cover the space left at the foot with another sheet.

Q. How should a patient be lifted on the night-chair?

The patient should clasp his hands round the neck of the sister, and in this position gently be moved along towards the chair.

Q. How should the patient be helped back to bed?

It can be managed in the same way: the patient being seated on the edge of the bed, the feet can be lifted from the floor with the right hand, and the body be supported with the left hand, and in this manner be brought into the right position.

Q. How can this be done if there are two persons?

Then one sister should place herself behind the patient and pass her arms under his arms, and clasp her hands over his chest. His head and shoulders will in this way rest against the sister's chest.

Q. How does the second sister take hold?

She clasps her hands under the patient's knees and raises them a little, then both lift him at the same moment and bring him into the desired position.

Q. How must this all be done?

This must all be done slowly and care must taken to put him down gently without any jar or twist.

Q. What should not be attempted if the patient is heavy?

Taking him out of the bed should not be attempted. In this case the bed pan or urinal should be used in place of the night-chair.

Arranging the Pillows.

Q. How should the pillows be placed?

They should be placed so as to raise the head and also to support the shoulders, so that the lungs can breath freely.

Q. What care must be taken in propping a patient up?

See that the first pillow is well pulled down to the small of the back. Commence with that pillow, and put the others each one behind the last.

Q. What will this prevent?

It will keep them from slipping.

Q. What is very important for the patient's comfort?

One or two small pillows or sofa-cushions, which can be covered with a linen case and moved about easily, just as any part needs a support.

The Manner of Bathing.

Q. What must be avoided in bathing.

Exposing and fatigueing the patient.

Q. What should be brought into the room?

Towels, soap, brushes, clean clothing and everything that is required.

Q. What should be avoided?

Going and coming, first fetching this, then that forgotten article. It makes the patient nervous.

Q. What should be spread on the bed?

A rubber sheet and folded sheet or draw sheet.

Q. How can the bath be given?

Slip the arms out of the sleeves, and then pass your hands under the bed clothes, using freely a warm, soapy cloth. The cloth should not be too wet, wring it out, and frequently dip it into the basin, and change the water once or twice.

Q. What may be done to cool and refresh the patient?.

Sponge face and hands several times a day.

Q. What may be put in the water?

A little cologne or alcohol, and a few drops of tr. of myrrh or cologne in the water, which should be given to wrinse out the mouth.

Q. What may be used in place of a tooth brush?

A soft linen cloth.

Plunge Bath.

Q. What kind of a bath tub is most convenient if the patient is able to take a plunge bath?

A portable bathtub which can be used at the bedside.

Q. Where and how must the bath be prepared if there is no portable bathtub?

Then the bath should be prepared in the bathroom, the temperature of the water and room must be tested with a thermometer, the room should be sufficiently warm to prevent any chill on emerging from the bath.

Q. How is the patient taken into the bath room?

The night clothes are removed before the patient leaves the bed, and a bathing apron is put on, or the patient is rolled in a sheet, then wrapped in a blanket and carried or wheeled into the bathroom.

Q. How is the patient put into the bath?

He is lifted into the bathtub, with the apron on or rolled in a sheet, for the length of time ordered by the doctor.

Q. What should be done on removing the patient from the bath?

He should be quickly wrapped in a warm dry sheet, then in a blanket and carried back to bed.

Q. Of what advantage is this manner for a weak patient?

In this way a weak patient can be made dry without extra fatigue; a little rubbing after he lies in bed is sufficient.

Q. How should he be rubbed?

With long strokes, not with little pats here and there?

Q. What is done after he is dry.

The damp sheet and blanket are removed and the night clothes put on.

Q. What should be done if a number of baths are ordered in one day?

Then it is best to roll the patient in a blanket, and not fatigue him with putting his night clothes off and on.

CHANGING OF NIGHT CLOTHES.

Q. How can the night clothes be changed?

Have everything ready at hand, well aired and warmed before you begin. Then you commence, in drawing the clothes, by slightly raising the patient, up under his back to the neck, and then slip them over his head.

Q. What makes this motion somewhat easier?

If it is possible for the patient to bend his head forward.

Q. What is taken off last?

The sleeves; if any part is afflicted this should be freed last from the clothes.

Q. How can it best be managed if the patient wears flannel shirts?

They should be open in front and slipped inside of the night gown, sleeves in sleeves, before beginning to make the change.

Q. How are the clean clothes put on?

The afflicted part is dressed first. If an arm or leg is afflicted, the sleeve should be ripped before it is put on.

Q. What makes a good protection for a patient?

A flannel sack put on the outside of the clean gown, and it should always be worn when there is much exposure.

FOOTBATH.

Q. How can you give a footbath?

Spread a rubber cloth over the sheet; have the water at the right temperature, tested by the elbow, to which it should feel hot; put the foot tub in the bed; place the patient on his back; draw up his knees and put the feet in water.

Q. What must be covered?

The knees and the tub must be covered with an extra blanket to keep the steam from the bed clothes.

COMBING THE HAIR.

Q. How can the pillows and bed be protected during the time the hair is combed?

By spreading a large towel or cloth about the patient.

Q. How should the hair be combed?

The hair should be lifted in locks, with one hand, and gently combed or brushed with the other.

Q. How should the hair never be fastened?

Never in a hard knot which presses on the patient's head while lying.

Q. How can the hair be arranged best?

In two braids.

BEDSORES.

Q. What is generally the cause of bedsores?

Bedsores are, in nine cases out of ten, the result of bad nursing. Prevention is better than cure.

Q. In order to prevent bedsores what must a sister not do?

She must not let false modesty prevent her from doing her duty in this matter. She should sponge the exposed parts, or those upon which pressure comes, daily with alcohol and water, dust them with starch and keep the under sheet perfectly dry and smooth, and clothing clean.

Q. What persons are very liable to have bedsores?

Very thin and very heavy persons, even without being very sick.

Q. How can pressure be avoided?

By changing the position of the patient every few hours and by using air pillows.

Q. What should be done as soon as red spots appear?

The affected parts should be at once attended to carefully, the alcohol bathing should be tried three or four times a day, followed by dusting with powder or bathed with the white of an egg and rainwater or brandy, and dusted with oxide of zinc.

Q. What should be tried if this fails to help?

Air or water bed, if it can be gotten.

Q. To whom must the red spots be shown?

To the doctor.

Q. What is generally discontinued after the skin is broken and what is applied?

The bathing of alcohol is discontinued, because its use is painful after the skin is broken. The sore place is frequently dressed with oxide of zinc or some other ointment prescribed by the doctor.

Q. What do neglected bedsores often do?

They part off from the sound flesh, and often lay bare the deeper tissues even to the bone.

Q. What is often used to separate the sloughing part?
Charcoal poultices.

Q. How long is this kept up?
Until the gangrenous portion is removed.

Q. How is the sore dressed and the dressing kept in place?
It is dressed antiseptically and the dressing kept in place with strips of adhesive plaster.

THE GIVING OF MEDICINE.

Q. How should medicine be given?
It should be given as near the exact time as possible, and the exact dose as ordered by the doctor.

Q. Is a sister allowed to trust her eye when giving medicine?
Never: she must measure it always in a graduated glass or drop it with care.

Q. How can medicine be given in drops?
The prescribed number of drops may be dropped on a lump of sugar or in a medicine glass or spoon. Wet the cork with the medicine and touch it to the mouth of the bottle at that place where the medicine is to be dropped out and by this prevent the medicine from flowing out too fast.

Q. What should every medicine bottle have?
A label with the exact direction of the doctor and the name of the patient.

Q. What will a trustworthy sister always do?
She will always look on the label of the bottle before taking the cork out, whether she thinks it is right or not. A good nurse should in this matter, as in all other things, acquire the habit of caution.

Q. On which side of the bottle should the medicine be poured out?
On the side opposite to the label, so as not to soil the label.

Q. What must be done immediately after the medicine is poured into the graduated glass?
The bottle must be corked at once.
Q. Why?
Otherwise the medicine will lose its strength.
Q. What should she do before she gives the medicine?
She must first look at the label on the bottle and then at the patient, to be sure that it is the patient for whom the medicine is prepared.
Q. If the sister neglects to give the medicine at the appointed time, what must she do?
If it is three minutes too late, she must ask the sister superior for permission to give the medicine; if it is five minutes too late, then she must ask mother superior's permission.
Q. What must be done every time after the medicine is given?
Every time after giving medicine, the sister must wash the medicine glass or spoon in a small bowl on the medicine waiter, and wipe them carefully.

THINGS IMPORTANT ENOUGH TO WRITE DOWN.

Q. What things should be written down by the nursing sister?
(1). The hours at which medicine is to be given, and each time when it is given, the hour to be crossed in the tablet.
(2). How much beef tea or milk the doctor has ordered for the patient.
(3). How often this nourishment should be given.
(4). How long intervals should be left between certain kinds of medicine and certain kinds of food.
Q. But what must be done if this is left to the discretion of the sister?
She must carefully arrange the time for giving food in such a way as not to destroy the patient's appetite by

giving medicine immediately before the food, or nauseate him by giving it too soon afterwards.

Q. What will a good nurse have for all these things?

She will have a well arranged time-table for all these things, written out for the day, and will need all her ingenuity and care to keep the hours of medicine and food exactly apart.

CLINICAL RECORD.

Q. What should be noted in the clinical record?

An exact account of what has taken place since the physician's last visit; how the temperature and pulse have varied and at what hours changes occurred; how often there has been a movement of the bowels, and what the character was; the character and quantity of urine passed; whether the sleep was quiet or restless; what, and at what hours, food and stimulants were taken; when medicines were given. In a word, all the symptoms the physician is interested to know, and that are of importance for him to know.

Q. What will this save?

All this, put plainly and in as few words as possible, in writing, will save a great deal of talking in the patient's room, and avoid anxiety on his part about his own symptoms.

Q. Of what benefit will it be for the doctor and also for the sister?

It will economize the doctor's time and will obviate mistakes if the sister should happen to be called away or is taking her necessary rest when the doctor calls, and some one else is in temporary charge.

Q. Why should a sister be so careful about these little things?

Because it is this systematic carefulness in these little things which makes the difference between a good nurse and a poor one.

Precautions on Leaving the Patient to Another's Care.

Q. What must a sister do if she is obliged to leave her patient in some other care for a while?

She must write down, what is to be done in her absence, the time for giving medicine or stimulants, or food, etc.

Q. How long may she stay?

No longer than the exact time provided for.

Q. What arrangements must the sister make in case she has to sleep?

She must arrange to be called at a certain hour. This is important, for the sister's mind must be relieved of anxiety about awakening.

Q. How should a sister always be towards a patient?

Kind and intelligent; he will then watch for her return, and prefer her to any one else.

Protecting the Patient.

Q. Against what must a sister protect her patient?

Against all, perhaps well-meaning, but injudicious interference.

Q. How can she do this?

By not allowing visits or conversations in his presence, that may injure or fatigue him, such as accounts of other people's diseases, or recommendations of sure cures and other quack treatments, etc.

Q. Who should be kept out of the sick room?

Thoughtless people and noisy children and as much as possible all visitors.

Q. Why?

Because the coming and going of visitors, chatting and questioning, fatigue, and are often injurious for the patient. Besides, the more persons are in a room, the less fresh air there is.

Q. What can a sister do in regard to keeping the patient quiet through the night?

By preventing him from hearing news, especially in the evening, or anything that may excite him. Keep his mind quiet for the night, and be very careful that his first sleep is not disturbed. A patient who is roused out of his first sleep, very often has his whole night's rest destroyed.

Q. What else is of great importance?

That no clock strikes during the night, in the room or hospital. Bells should be covered, so that they cannot be heard through the whole house and disturb the patient every time it rings, for it is cruel to disturb the sleep of a poor invalid, even for a minute, without absolute necessity.

Q. What must the sister be especially careful about in regard to bad news?

If during the illness bad news of any kind has come to the family, she must not allow it to be told to the patient without the doctor's permission. Under no circumstances should the patient be suddenly shocked or pained by such communications.

Q. What else must the sister do that the patient be not disturbed at night?

She should make all the arrangements for the night early, have the fire in order, the different articles needed at night at hand, the room aired, the last medicine and food promptly given, the bedside table ready, and the light turned down and shaded from the eyes of the patient. Tin shields are best for gasburners.

FOOD AT NIGHT.

Q. What patients must be fed at night?

With very sick patients medicine and feeding go on regularly during the twenty-four hours, day and night. Besides these, all patients suffering from exhaustion or slowly recovering from a wearing illness, should take some light and nourishing food just before retiring.

Q. What may be given?

A glass of milk, not to cold, a cup of gruel, or a cup of well-made beef tea, will support the patient through the night, and prevent the feeling of exhaustion in the morning.

Q. If a patient is very ill, at what time will he need the closest attention?

Toward morning: for at this period of the lowest temperature the fatal chill often occurs, and the patient may be lost from the want of a little external warmth.

Q. What should be done if such is the case?

The fire should, if necessary, be replenished, the feet and legs should be kept warm, and whenever a tendency to chilling is discovered, hot bottles, hot bricks or warm flannels, with some warm drink, should be made use of until the temperature is restored.

Q. What should be provided for towards morning, even in case the patient is not very ill?

Some light nourishment. The patient has perhaps been restless and wakeful, or is exhausted by heavy sleep, or is feeble from old age, or convalescing from severe sickness, with the longing for food, which is sometimes felt on recovery from fever.

Q. When should this be provided for and where should it be kept?

It should be provided for, the evening before, and not wait until breakfast time. It should be had on hand in some accessible place, not in the patient's, or any other occupied room.

Q. What nourishment would do in this case?

A cup of gruel, beef tea, coffee or milk, or anything which the patient is allowed to eat, and that can be heated on a spirit lamp or gas stove.

Q. What should be done before the patient takes this?

The patient's mouth should first be washed out with a soft cloth, or water given him to wrinse out his mouth.

The Nursing Sister.

Q. What is often the effect of this morning nourishment?

The patient will often have a refreshing morning nap.

Q. Should any cooking be done in the sickroom?

Never, if it can possibly be helped. All warming should be done either in the adjoining room or in the kitchen, but never in the presence of the patient.

The Proper Manner of Serving Meals.

Q. How should the meals be served to the patient?

Serve them upon a tray or a bedtray, which is covered with a clean napkin. Have cups and spoons shining and clean. Be careful not to slop the tea into the saucer, and bring too much of anything.

Q. What should the sister be especially careful about?

That all necessary things are on the tray when it is brought to the patient. If she is obliged to go for something forgotten, she should never set the waiter on the bed, but on the table.

Q. What should the sister never do in the presence of the patient?

Never taste the food.

Q. What must be done as soon as the patient has eaten his meals?

The tray should at once be taken out of the room.

Q. Should any food be kept in the sickroom?

No. A cup of beef tea which may be soon needed can be kept in the nearest cool place, carefully covered. The ledge outside the window in the shade, will answer, if there be no better place, but never on a window facing the front of a hospital. It should be taken away from the bed even if you have to give it in ten minutes again.

Q. Where should medicine, food and stimulants never be kept?

Never where the patient can see or smell them. Food should never be left standing on the table with the idea that perhaps the patient will take little by little. If the patient wishes anything, it should be brought promptly, hot or cold, the right quantity, quietly, without too much stir.

FEEDING A PATIENT.

Q. How can you feed a patient?

Prop him up gently; in cold weather put something around his shoulders, and a napkin under his chin and over the sheet. Do this whenever anything is put in his mouth.

Q. What should a sister avoid and what should she notice while feeding the patient?

She should not hurry the patient and avoid talking to him while he is eating. Notice the quantity taken, and report to the doctor in definite terms. For instance, he took four tablespoons full of soup or a wineglass of punch, etc.

Q. What must a sister consult regarding nourishment?

The hours when the patient can best take his food; she must try to prevent faintness by all means.

Q. What has been the consequence of neglect in this matter?

Not few lives are lost by mere starvation, where a little ingenuity and a great deal of perseverence might have averted the result.

Q. If a patient feels faint at a certain time one day, how can this be prevented the following day?

By giving him the beef tea or stimulants just before that time the following day.

Q. How can you pursuade the patient to eat?

Bring the food, whatever it is, to him. Do not say, "Don't you think you can take a little of this or that, unless you have it in your hands at the time; the patient will get over the fancy for it while you are gone to prepare it.

Q. What should be done regarding diet?

It should be varied as much as possible, when allowed, but with a very sick patient do not use up what little appetite or power or digestion there may be, with foolish things, viz.: jelly or other sweets.

Q. How can you feed a helpless patient?

By giving him his food in manageable mouthfuls, and not hurrying. When he has finished, wipe or wash the mouth gently, take away the bed-rest, and let the patient down slowly with your hand under the pillows.

Q. What should be done if the patient cannot take much food at a time?

In such a case give food frequently at short intervals.

Q. Should the patient be waked for food in such a case?

Ask the doctor about that. Sleep is sometimes more important than food. Great care must be taken not to interrupt the sleep unnecessarily.

Q. What should be remembered at the same time?

That patients sometimes sink away in their sleep, whilst if they had been roused and fed they might have lived. Six small meals are better for most sick people than three large ones.

Q. How can you feed a delirious patient?

Rouse the patient's attention as much as possible, call him by his name, press the spoon against the lower lip, and move it gently back and forth.

Q. What will generally be the consequence?

The lips will part involuntarily, and then the spoon should be passed in, far back in the mouth, and emptied slowly. The patient must be slightly raised by a hand under the pillow.

Q. What do unconscious patients often suffer from?

From thirst, and must therefore have water given to them from time to time, or the tongue and mouth become very dry and the breathing more difficult.

OBSERVATION OF SYMPTOMS.

Q. What distincts a trained nurse from an untrained one?

A great point of distinction between a trained nurse and an untrained one is the ability of the former to observe accurately and describe intelligibly what comes under her notice in the sick room.

Q. Why is this point so very important?

Because a nurse who is constantly with the patient or around him has a much better opportunity of becoming acquainted with his real condition than the physician, who perhaps spends only one-half hour or less with him occasionally, that is, if she knows how to observe and report symptoms correctly and distinctly.

Q. What does the visit of the physician often cause?

The very excitement of this visit will often temporarily change the entire aspect of the patient and make him appear better or worse than he really is.

Q. What must the physician know in order to form a correct judgment about the case?

He must know what goes on in his absence, as well as in his presence, and for such information he is forced to rely almost wholly upon the sister.

Q. What is, therefore, of the greatest importance?

That the sister cultivates the habit of a critical observation, and simple, direct, truthful statement. Even where there is no intention to deceive, very few persons are capable of making a report of anything which shall neither be deficient, exaggerated or perverted.

Q. What does the doctor want to know from a sister?

He wants to know facts, not opinions, and a nurse who can tell him exactly what has happened, without obscuring it in a cloud of generalities, hasty interferences, or second hand information, will be recognized as an invaluable assistant.

Q. How are symptoms classified?

Subjective, viz.: those which are evident only to the patient; and objective, viz.: which may be conceived by outside observers and simulated, feigned for purpose of deceit, either to excite sympathy, or from other motives.

Q. What is required to be able to distinguish between real and feigned symptoms?

It requires both experience and judgment. For it may happen that an expert villain (malingerer) will now and then deceive doctors and sisters into the treatment of a malady, that has no real existence, while on the other hand genuine suffering may chance to be mistaken for fraud or hysteria, if the usual objective manifestations are absent.

Q. What cases are always more or less suspicious?

Those that are entirely subjective (that is, where symptoms are only evident to the patient), as diseases unaccompanied by any outward sign are comparatively rare.

Q. What must be done before an opinion is passed in regard to true or deceitful symptoms?

The patient must be closely watched without him noticing it, for it is better to be duped once in a while than to fail to give aid or sympathy where it is really needed. The sister should let nothing pass unseen, and note the most fleeting signs. By doing this she can soon judge to some extent, whether his statements are to be relied upon, and whether he has a tendency to exaggerate his ills, or to make light of them.

Q. To whom does the decision of the existence of a disease solely belong?

To the doctor, but he will be largely guided by the observations of the attentive sister, and she herself will often be called upon to judge as to the urgency of special indications.

Q. What may a sister be called upon to judge?

Whether she shall send for the doctor in the middle of the night, or apply her own resources, whether she should give or withhold the medicine left to be used only in emergency, or whether she should alter or let alone any arrangement which has proved unexpectedly uncomfortable.

Q. What position does a sufferer take?

Instinctively the position most calculated for ease?

Q. How does the patient generally lay when one lung is affected?

The patient then lays on that side, so that the healthy one, which has to do the most work, may have the greatest freedom of motion.

Q. What position suggests peritonitis?

Lying on the back, with the knees drawn up so as to relax the abdominal muscles.

Q. What position does a patient take in colic?

You may find the patient lying on the abdomen, as pressure relieves pain of such character.

Q. What may be looked upon as a sign of improvement?

If a patient who has been lying persistently on his back, turns over to his side.

Q. What is a sure sign that the distress of difficulty in breathing is removed?

If the patient, who has been forced to sit up, lies down and composes for sleep.

Q. In what cases does this inability to breathe occur?

In cases where the lungs or heart are affected.

Q. What is usually a favorable sign?

Lying quietly, but in acute rheumatism the patient is quiet because the least motion causes him pain. Again extreme weakness may render it too great an exertion to move.

Q. When does restlessness occur?

Restlessness is ominous in most organic diseases?

Q. What is sometimes a very bad sign?

Slipping down in bed.

Q. Which are the most important indices of a disease?

Pulse, respiration and temperature are sometimes called the three vital signs.

Q. What should be observed about the pulse?

The frequency and force.

Q. What should be observed about the respirations?

The rate, any peculiarities, whether it is abdominal or thoric, if regular or irregular, easy or labored, and whether or not accompanied by pain.

Q. In what case is lung disease accompanied by pain, and when not?

There is no pain in diseases of the lung substance alone; when the pleura is affected, then there is a sharp pain.

Q. By what are most disorders of the respiratory organs accompanied?

By a cough.

Q. What is this caused by?

By an irritation of the air passage, and is often the effort of expulsion of some foreign matter.

Q. What is the matter coughed up called?

Sputa.

.Q What is a cough said to be if not accompanied by expectoration?

A dry cough.

Q. How is the expectoration generally in the bronchitis?

First simply mucus, later pus; in chronic cases it is thick and yellow.

Q. How is it in consumption?

At first very tenacious, sometimes frothy; at an advanced stage pus with streaks of blood, sometimes peculiar cheesy lumps are expectorated.

Q. How in pneumonia?

In pneumonia it is for the most part scanty; after a certain stage it has a rusty color.

Q. What is the character in gangrene of the lungs?

Dark greenish sputa, very free and offensive.

Q. How in cancer of the lungs?

A peculiar gelatinous form.

Q. What more should be observed about the cough?

Whether it is worst in daytime or nighttime, if it is first increased by moving about or on first waking, whether hard or loose, choking, hard or incessant.

Q. What should be done if a patient complains of cold without apparent reason?

Take the temperature.

Q. What does a sense of coldness along the spine often signify?

A chill, and the temperature will be found rather elevated than lowered. Although the patient shivers, the temperature rises, because the small blood-vessels (capillaries) are so contracted that the blood cannot get to the surface to be cooled.

Q. What always follows a genuine chill?
High fever.

Q. When should the temperature be taken?
During and after the chill.

Q. What should be carefully noted?
The time of occurrence of the chill, duration and number.

Q. What often accompanies the fall of febrile temperature?
Free perspiration.

Q. What else can produce this perspiration?
Extreme weakness.

Q. Is the moisture or dryness of the skin important?
Yes, it is always important. A high fever with a wet skin is more alarming than the same temperature with dry skin.

Q. What should be noticed about the perspiration?
In what part of the body the moisture appears, at what time, in connection with what symptoms, whether it is cold or warm, and if there is any peculiar odor about it.

Q. What certain symptoms are often found in pulmonary diseases?
A high color on one cheek alone.

Q. What does a sudden change of color give a warning for?
It gives warning for fainting (syncope).

Q. What accompanies internal hemorrhage?
Extreme paleness.

Q. What indicates nausea?

Paleness about the mouth, with compressed or slightly paled lips.

Q. What should especially be noticed?

Any eruption or rash; this must be promptly reported, its character, location, extent, time of appearance.

Q. What should be noticed about the tongue?

Whether it is dry or coated, or swollen.

Q. How is the tongue likely to be in fever?

Furred.

Q. Is a furred tongue always a sign of disease?

No; for some people have a furred tongue in good health, or it is induced by slight constipation.

Q. What opportunity should be taken in looking at the tongue?

Notice the odor of the breath and the state of the teeth and gums.

Q. What must be looked out for, while calomel or other medicine containing mercury, is given?

For looseness of the teeth and sore gums.

Q. What is this soreness called?

Salivated.

Q. What is a very common symptom?

Nausea.

Q. How is it usually reliev.d?

By vomiting.

Q. What should be noted about vomiting?

Whether it is persistently accompanied by straining or pain, the intervals since taking food or medicine, the amount vomited and the character.

Q. What will generally be the character?

Undigested food; it may contain bile, blood or even faecal matter.

Q. What may the vomiting of faecal matter indicate?

This is an important symptom and may indicate intestinal obstruction, and may call for immediate operation.

Q. What effect have some drugs, as iron and bismuth, upon stools?

They blacken the stools.

Q. What color are the stools in jaundice?

Very light clay-colored.

Q. What is important to note about stools?

Frequency and quantity of the evacuation, if solid or fluid, the presence of mucus, pus, blood or worms.

Q. What should be done if there is any doubt about the character of the stools?

It should be saved for the doctor's inspection.

Q. What is always more or less important?

Hemmorrhage from any organ. Even a slight nose-bleed may be an initial symptom of a typhoid.

Q. What must be carefully observed?

The color, quantity and general character.

Q. What should be noted in regard to pain?

Whether it is acute, dull, aching, stinging, burning, steady, spasmodic, etc.

Q. What should be done if it is uncertain whether a circumstance is of any value?

It should be noted, for it is better to report to the physician a dozen superfluous items, than to omit one of importance. Memory should never be trusted, but everything written down.

BEDMAKING.

Q. What is one of the most important daily duties of a sister of charity?

The making of the bed.

Q. What does the good making up of a bed impart to the patient?

It imparts a great relief to the patient if his bed is arranged and made up well.

Q. How should you make up a bed for a patient who is not very ill?

(1). To make up the bed for a patient, who is able and allowed to leave the bed, you first help the patient out of bed, and place him well propped, and protected with covers against taking cold in a chair, near the bed.

(2). Take the bedclothes one by one out of the bedstead and shake them up well.

Q. What shall be done if the bed has a strawsack?

It shall be shaken up well, if anything is soiled it must be removed and the pillows arranged in the proper way.

Q. What must be done if the bed has a mattress and bolster?

They must be turned every day.

Q. What is to be done with soiled sheets?

Soiled sheets should be removed and replaced by clean ones, which are to be spread straight and smooth upon the bed, to prevent bedsores.

Q. What must be put in the bed of a patient who passes the discharges into the bed?

In such a case it is necessary that a rubber sheet and a draw sheet be placed in the bed.

Q. How shall the sheets be kept straight?

By tucking them securely under the mattress or strawsack.

Q. How is the top sheet turned?

The upper sheet is turned down over the cover, and then turned down with the covers towards the foot end of the bed.

Q. How is the patient then brought back to bed?

The patient is then brought carefully and easy to bed.

Q. What care must be taken in regard to covers by patients with fever?

That they are not covered in an unreasonable manner with heavy covers.

Q. What is to be done if it is impossible for the patient to sit up?

Such patients are placed on a couch or stretcher.

Q. What is required when a patient is to be laid upon a stretcher?

To raise a patient carefully from his bed, and put him on a stretcher, or change him from one bed to another, it requires several sisters and certain manipulations.

Q. Where is the stretcher placed, when a patient is to be placed upon it?

The stretcher is set near the side of the bed, so that the head end of the stretcher stands even with the foot end of the bed.

Q. How is the patient lifted upon it?

(1). One of the sisters clasps the head and shoulders of the patient, while the patient supports his hands and arms on the shoulder of the sister.

(2). Another sister clasps the hips, a third the knees and limbs.

Q. When and how is the patient lifted?

All three lift the patient at the same time, make a turn, so that the position of his head corresponds with the head end of the stretcher.

Q. How should the patient be lowered?

The patient should be lowered easy and gently.

Q. In what way should the patient be put back to bed?

In the same manner as he was brought from the bed to the stretcher. This is also to be observed, when the patient is to be brought into the bathtub.

Laying Out a Corpse.

Q. What is to be observed when laying out a corpse?

The same tenderness and modesty is to be observed as with a living patient.

Q. Why?

Although the body is dead and without feeling, it is venerable, when looked upon in the light of faith, for it was once a temple of the Holy Ghost.

Q. How should you, therefore, never handle the body?

One should never handle the body roughly; always lift it with two or three persons, if it is heavy; never let the head fall, and never step in or over the coffin.

Q. What can be done so as not to be disturbed by the family?

In order not to be disturbed, you can lock the door ten or fifteen minutes.

Q. What must a sister provide for?

A sister must take care that she has sufficient confidential assistance, especially by grown persons.

Q. How should the corpse be prepared?

The face, the eyes, the ears, nose, mouth and teeth must be washed as clean as possible, the hair combed neatly.

Q. How should hands and feet be cleaned?

The hands and arms should at least be washed thoroughly up to the elbows, the fingernails trimmed. The feet are also thorougly washed, the toe-nails trimmed and cleaned.

Q. What is to be done after the corpse is washed?

After the body is washed, clean clothes are put on, whereat the utmost modesty must be preserved and is only done under the covers.

Q. What is laid upon the eyes?

Small square pieces of linen, folded several times, dipped in some liquid, so that the eyes remain closed.

Q. What is tied around the mouth?

A thin, white cloth is tied tight around it.

Q. In what position are the hands placed if the deceased was a Catholic?

The hands are folded as for prayer.

Q. What should the sisters pray who assist at laying out a corpse?

The fourth penitential psalm.

Q. How shall they pray it?

In a low tone, so as not to disturb others.

Q. What should never be dropped carelessly?
Neither the coffin itself, nor the handles.

CLEANING OF THE ROOMS AND CORRIDORS.

1. Dusting.

Q. When should a room be dusted?
The room should be dusted after sweeping and before mopping.

Q. With what should it be done?
It can be done with two dusting cloths, by first dusting with one and then using the other, or with one dusting cloth and a hairbrush.

Q. What should never be used for dusting?
Featherdusters.

Q. For what reason?
Because they only serve to whirl the dust around in the room, but do not remove it, and therefore act very injuriously upon the lungs.

Q. If the washstand and the small table at the head of the bed is covered with an oilcloth, how can it be kept clean?
They must be washed off daily, likewise the articles which are upon the washstand.

2. Mopping the Room.

Q. How can a room be thoroughly cleaned?
If the room is to be mopped, all furniture, tables, chairs, etc., are moved from their places, or, if possible, carried out of the room, then wipe up to the washboard with a clean, soft cloth.

Q. How is the floor mopped?
The floor is mopped with a coarse mop rag and a stick, but great care must be taken, not to touch the washboard, and thereby spoil the paint.

Q. How should you wring out the cloth?

The first time it should be fairly wet, the second time wring it out tight and rub it over the floor vigorously.

Q. What should never be left standing after mopping?

Pools of water.

CLEANING THE PATIENT.

1. Washing.

Q. How can a patient be washed?

If the patient is not too weak, and can sit up, then he is washed while he is sitting up, and also combed.

Q. With what is the patient generally washed?

Face and hands are generally washed with tepid water.

Q. In what cases must this be omitted?

If the patient is afflicted with rash, erysipelis, measles, scarlet fever, smallpox, etc.

2. Bathing.

Q. What directions must be followed at bathing the patient?

The doctor's directions must be strictly followed.

Q. How are baths distinguished?

We distinguish full baths, or local baths, that is bathing certain parts of the body.

Q. How is a full or plunge bath given?

If the patient has enough strength to walk he will go to the bathroom and take his bath there precisely as prescribed by the doctor in regard to temperature, time and mixture.

Q. How are weak patients taken to the bathroom?

Very weak patients are undressed in bed, a bathing apron or gown put on, wrapped in a blanket, and carefully placed with the apron into the bath.

Q. What shall be given to weak patients before the bath?

Weak patients should always take a stimulant before the bath.

Q. What is to be done if the patient should faint while bathing?

If the patient should nevertheless faint, the bath must at once be interrupted and the case must be reported to the doctor.

Q. What is to be done after the bath?

Immediately after the bath the patient must be well rubbed and brought to bed, and, if necessary, some refreshments given.

3. Changing the Clothes.

Q. How should a sister change the clothes and underwear of a patient?

To change the clothes of a patient it requires great care and practice.

Q. How can a nightgown or shirt be changed?

If a nightgown or shirt is to be changed, then lift the patient slightly, draw the shirt or gown up under the back up to the neck and then over the head.

Q. What is stripped off last?

The sleeves.

Q. If the arm be the afflicted part what care must be taken?

Care must be taken that the afflicted part be released from the clothes last.

Q. How are the clean clothes put on the patient?

In putting on the clean clothes, the reverse is followed from the taking off, namely, the afflicted part is taken first.

VENTILATION.

Q. In what does the proper ventilation of a room consist?

The proper ventilation of a room consists in trying constantly to renew the used and foul air, through fresh air from outdoors.

Q. What can be done for this purpose?

For this purpose keep the window farthest from the patient, day and night, down at least an inch from the top, so that fresh air can constantly come in.

Q. What shall be done besides this?

Besides this the windows should be opened wide three times a day, morning, noon and evening, in dry weather.

Q. What special care should be taken during this time?

Care must be taken that the patient is protected from draught, by covering and keeping him covered with extra blankets until the temperature again rises to 68 or 70 degrees after ventilating.

Q. Is ventilation of great importance in hospitals?

Yes: ventilation of halls and rooms in a hospital is of the greatest importance.

Q. Why?

Because fresh air is half the medicine, while foul air is almost poison.

Q. What is therefore one of the most important duties of a nurse?

To be just as conscientious about ventilating as about giving medicine and performing other important duties.

Q. How can the ventilation in a hospital be best regulated?

An intelligent and prudent sister should be appointed in every house, who has to attend to the ventilation in the whole house three times a day in the rooms, with the above mentioned precautions.

Q. Is it enough to ventilate the halls three times a day?

No; the halls should be ventilated more frequently, at least five times a day, especially then when on account of bad weather the ventilation in the rooms is impossible through the open window.

Temperature of the Room.

Q. What besides the bedstead and table is an absolute necessary article in the sick room.

A thermometer for the regulating of the temperature of the room.

Q. How should the temperature be kept?

The temperature should be kept equal, never below 65 degrees and never above 70 degrees.

Q. How can this heat be replaced in winter?

In winter the temperature must be replaced through artificial heat, as stove, water, air or steam heat.

Q. Of what advantage is an open fireplace in a sickroom?

If an open fireplace can be had in a sickroom, it will serve a double purpose, affording the necessary heat and ventilation.

Q. What special care should be taken in summer time?

In summer, care should be taken to exclude the rays of the sun, through rouleaux or blinds, and by sprinkling water or ether to remove the close air.

Taking Temperature.

Q. What is the normal temperature of the human body?

The normal temperature is 98 4-10 degrees.

Q. How is the temperature taken if the patient is awake and conscious?

Then it is safest to put the thermometer in the mouth.

Q. How is the thermometer placed in the mouth?

It is placed in the mouth beneath the tongue, the lips closed for 3 to 5 minutes.

Q. In what case should the thermometer never be placed in the mouth?

It should never be placed in the mouth if the patient is not wide awake, or if he is irresponsible, for then there is danger that he may break the thermometer by biting it, and this would cause immediate danger of life.

Q. Where should the thermometer be placed in this case?

In this case the thermometer should be placed under the clothes, in the patient's axilla, between the upper arm and the chest, while the arm is closely pressed to the chest.

Q. How long should the thermometer remain in the axilla?

At least five minutes.

Q. When is the temperature generally taken?

The temperature is generally taken in the morning at 8 and in the evening at 6 o'clock.

Q. In what cases is the temperature to be taken more frequently?

In cases of typhoid fever the temperature is taken more frequently, according to the directions of the doctor.

Q. On what shall the clinical thermometer be kept and brought to the room?

It should be kept on a small waiter or plate with clean sponge, small bottle or glass of a weak solution of carbolic acid, and a clock or watch with a minute hand.

Q. For what purpose is the carbolized solution used?

For washing the thermometer before and after using it.

Q. What shall be put in the bottom of the bottle?

A little cotton to avoid breaking the thermometer in case it slips and strikes the bottom.

Q. How often should this solution be changed?

Twice a week.

BANDAGING.

Q. What is the first thing to be shown in bandaging instruction?

To roll a bandage by hand.

Q. How is it done?

It is taken into the right hand, the end of the strip is folded over upon itself, until you have a little roll stiff enough to keep in shape.

Q. In which hand is the roll taken?

It is taken into the right hand between the thumb and middle finger. Then turn it, let the bandage pass over the back of the left hand, between the forefinger and thumb, and be pressed with the thumb of the other hand against the roll.

Q. With what part of the human body should the teacher begin this instruction?

First with the hand, then with the arm.

Q. How long should this be practiced?

Until every novice has acquired a facility to make and reverse the bandages, and the reverses are even and straight.

Q. What next?

Then the elbow is bandaged, the upper arm, the single and double shoulder-brace, the fingers, the foot, the heel, finally the head and the eyes.

Q. What are bandages used for?

To hold the dressings in place, to give support, or prevent motion.

Q. How shall a bandage be removed?

A bandage must be removed with the greatest care, without hurry, without jerking, so that the afflicted part is not concussed, which would cause the patient pain, or hemorrhage, or dislocate a set fracture.

Q. What must be done if the bandage adheres to the wound?

In that case it must be moistened with an antiseptic solution to loosen it.

Q. What bandages are commonly used?

Roller bandages, many-tailed bandages and T Bandages.

Q. What are roller bandages?

They are strips of muslin, flannel or gauze from half an inch to eight inches wide and of different length, tightly rolled upon themselves.

Q. What must be trimmed off the bandages?
Loose threads and the selvages.
Q. What kind of a bandage must be used for moist or wet dressings?
Of material that has been washed before.
Q. Why?
Because inconvenience may arise from shrinkage.
Q. How can bandages be pieced?
Lay the two flat ends on each other, overlapping for an inch, sew with long stitches.
Q. How should it be rolled?
As tight as possible.
Q. How should you unwind the bandage in putting on a roller bandage?
No faster than necessary, keeping the roll close to the body.
Q. How must a well-fitting bandage lie?
Smooth, without wrinkles, making an even pressure.
Q. How must they be applied?
Not too loose, or it will slip off, and not too tight, or it will be painful and impede the circulation.
Q. What bandage is used when it is important to avoid motion?
A many-tailed bandage.
Q. Of what is this made?
Of a piece of muslin torn into strips from each side to within an inch or two of the center.
Q. What bandage is an improvement upon this?
The bandage of Scultetus.
Q. How can this be made?
Take a long strip of muslin, sew across it at right angles other strips overlapping each other by two-thirds their width.
Q. What other bandage is frequently used?
A "T" bandage, being called so because it has the form of the Roman letter T.

Q. What is a sling or triangular bandage?
It is either a square or three-cornered piece of muslin.

Q. What are rubber bandages used for?
To reduce or prevent swelling.

Q. How should they be put on?
Without any reverses, and special care must be taken to avoid getting them too tight.

Q. What besides these may be used for the same purpose?
An elastic stocking is usually used in case of varicose veins.

Q. What is another means of affording support or protection to a limb or other parts?
By strapping with adhesive plaster.

Q. How must the strips be cut?
Lengthwise.

Q. How can they be warmed if necessary?
By holding the plain side over a flame or hot water.

Q. What must be done with the part or limb to which the plaster is to be applied?
It must be thoroughly cleaned and shaved.

Q. In what cases is strapping employed in the place of bandaging?
In cases of fractured ribs, or whenever it is desirable to limit the movements of the chest.

Q. What advantage has strapping?
It can be employed to one side only.

Q. How are plaster of paris bandages made?
They are prepared by rubbing into coarse gauze or muslin rollers as much of the plaster of paris as they will carry.

Q. Where must they be kept if they are not used at once?
In tin boxes.

Q. What kind of plaster of paris bandages are mostly used at the present time?
Such as are bought already prepared, and packed each one alone in air-tight tin boxes.

Q. What must be done with the limb before the plaster of paris cast is put on?

It must be thoroughly cleaned, and, if necessary, shaved, then a soft stocking or piece of soft flannel wrapped around it.

Q. What is done with the bandage before it is applied?

As soon as the doctor is ready it is emersed into water until well saturated, then squeezed out and handed to the doctor.

Q. What adds to setting of plaster of paris?

A little salt put in the water.

Q. Is the salt always used?

No; some surgeons say it spoils the cast; follow the directions of the surgeon.

Q. How long does it generally take before they are perfectly dry?

About twelve hours, more or less, according to thickness.

Q. What is required when a plaster of paris jacket is applied?

A frame, in which the patient can be placed so that the feet do not touch the floor.

Q. What is put on the patient before the bandages are applied?

A thin, tight-fitting woven undershirt.

Q. How long must the broken limb be kept perfectly quiet, after applying the plaster bandages?

Until the cast is firm.

Q. What may be used to keep it in position?

Sandbags filled about three-quarters full of fine sand.

Q. What will they hasten if they are heated?

The drying.

Q. When a plaster splint is to be removed, what will facilitate the process?

By moistening it along the proposed line of incision with diluted hydrochloric acid.

Q. How long is the cast left on?

Until the fracture is healed, or as long as the afflicted part needs a support.

Q. With what is it taken off?

With a small saw or scissors made for this purpose.

Q. What is necessary, if there is a wound beneath the plaster cast?

That a piece of the plaster is cut out, so that the secretion can escape and the wound be dressed.

Q. What must a sister get ready when a plaster of paris cast is to be applied?

Warm and cold water, plaster of paris bandages, dry plaster of paris, aprons, towels, and, if needed, a frame and a stocking sleeve or undershirt.

Night Watching.

Q. What is night watching?

Night watching is to watch by and nurse the patient during the hours of night.

Q. Is it necessary?

It is absolutely necessary if the patient is very ill; it belongs to the regular arrangements and duties of a hospital.

Q. At what time does the first night nurse come on duty?

The first night nurse comes on duty at 8 o'clock and remains until half past twelve in the morning.

Q. The second?

The second comes on at half past twelve and remains until half past five.

Q. What kind of shoes should the night nurse wear and for what reason?

The night nurse wears soft shoes instead of leather ones, so she may move quietly about in the whole house.

Q. If a sister has a special night watch where should she remain?

She should then constantly remain in the room or at the bed of the patient.

Q. How should a sister manage if she has the night watch in the male or female department, or in the wards?

In this case the sister makes her rounds in the wards assigned to her every hour or oftener if necessary, and watches whether there is anything to do.

Q. How must she move about?

The sister must move about quietly, without a light, open the door carefully, cast a glance over the entire ward.

Q. If everything is quiet and the patients asleep, what should the sister do?

The sister should shut the door slowly, without any noise and withdraw.

Q. If there are some very ill patients in a ward, what should a sister do then?

If there are some very ill patients who do not require a special night watch, the sister should go up to the bed and observe the patient for a few minutes.

Q. What should the sister do if he is asleep?

The sister should then not disturb him. If he wishes anything, he'll surely ask for it.

Q. What is of special importance at night?

It is very important at night that the doors be opened and shut without making a noise.

Q. If any door should make a noise, what is to be done?

It must be arranged in daytime, so that the sleep of the patients is not disturbed during the night.

Q. If the patient has taken anything to sleep, shall he be disturbed to take other medicine?

No; this would not only be imprudent, but cruel. In this case, the sister should wait until the patient wakes up.

Q. In what case is the patient to be waked up to take other medicine?

Only in special cases, when the doctor has ordered it.

Q. What patients often have to be awakened to take nourishment or stimulants?

Fever patients or very weak patients, or convalescents, if they sleep sound too long, may be awakened, to give them a drink or stimulants, provided the doctor has ordered it.

FOOD.

Q. Whose directions has the sister to follow in regard to nourishment and food for the patient?

Food should be given according to the directions of the doctor as to quality, quantity and time.

Q. Must this rule always be observed?

All sisters are bound to observe this rule strictly.

Q. If this rule is not followed, what might be the consequence?

There is great danger that the sisters will injure the patient.

Q. How should the meals be brought to a patient?

Whoever brings the meals to a patient, should see that there is a clean napkin on the waiter, that glasses, plates, dishes, cups, knives, spoons and forks are perfectly clean and bright.

GIVING MEDICINE.

Q. What are the duties of the sister who distributes the medicine?

The sister who gives the medicine to the patients, must be especially conscientious and give it exactly at the prescribed hour, and also in the prescribed quantity.

Q. As to the quantity, is she allowed to depend upon the eye?

She is not allowed to depend upon the eye, but should use a graduated glass for this purpose every time.

Q. Why should she use a graduated glass or spoon?

Because common teaspoons and tablespoons are of such varying sizes that it is unsafe to trust to them in measuring doses.

Q. Can a sister be too exact in this matter?

It is not possible to be too exact; for to judge of the right quantity of doses by the eye is a crime.

ATOMIZER.

Q. When is a hand-atomizer used?

In cases where it is necessary to throw a spray into the mouth, throat, etc. The prescribed fluid is either hot or cold.

Q. Is there any other atomizer?

Yes; steam atomizers.

Q. What care must be taken when a steam atomizer is used?

Not to have too much or too little water in the kettle.

Q. For what reason?

Because if there be too much water, the hot water would boil out and scald the patient's mouth, and if not enough the kettle would burst.

BEDREST.

Q. If there is no bedrest at hand, what can be used in its place?

Take a high, flat-backed chair, turn it up in such a way that the four feet are in the air, and that it rests on the edge of the seat and top of the back.

Q. How should the patient be supported?

Slip the back of the chair down in the bed, well covered with pillows filled in to the small of the patient's back, and supporting his back and shoulders.

Q. In what case is a regularly made bedrest necessary?

When the patient is permanently feeble, then a bedrest which can be lowered and raised is necessary, and it should have arms or braces to keep the patient from slipping down on either side.

CATHETERS.

Q. How many different kind of catheters are used?

Three: glass, rubber or silver ones.

Q. In what way are the rubber ones the best?

They are flexible and least likely to hurt or injure the patient.

Q. What size of rubber catheters are generally used for female patients?

Number seven.

Q. Which are the cleanest?

The glass ones.

Q. How are the glass ones kept antiseptic?

Immediately after they are used they should be washed with clear water, then laid in cold or warm water (not hot) and set on the stove to boil for about five minutes. Then they are again washed with sterilized water and kept in a covered glass bottle or jar, which contains an antiseptic solution, either of carbolic acid or bichloride. In this way they are always ready for use.

Q. What should be kept at the bottom of the glass?

Some cotton, so that if the catheter should happen to slip it would not strike the bottom of the glass, and by this prevent breaking of the catheter.

Q. How are the rubber ones cleaned?

They must be washed thoroughly immediately after they are used, with green soap or sapolio and hot water, and let plenty of hot water run through the catheter. Then wipe it dry and keep it wrapped in a piece of gauze.

Q. When must the rubber ones be boiled?

In certain cases when the doctor requires it, always before using it from one patient to another.

Q. Where can they be kept if they are used at short intervals?

In a weak solution of carbolic acid?

Q. How are the silver ones cleaned?

They are cleaned and boiled in the same way as the glass ones, then wiped and laid aside.

Q. What catheters should be oiled before they are used?

The flexible rubber and the silver ones.

Q. How can this be done?

After they are drawn through a carbolized solution, then through sterilized water, they are oiled with the finger. Never put the instrument into the vaseline, for this might close up the opening in the instrument and also mix the vaseline with the urine and render it unfit for examination.

Q. What must the sister do before she uses the catheter?

After having washed her hands thoroughly she must lock the door, or, if in a ward, place a screen around the bed, remove the covers with exception of the sheets. In some cases it will be necessary to wash her hands in an antiseptic solution or sterilized water.

Q. How should the catheter be used?

Have the patient flat on the back, if possible with the thighs slightly separated. Then wash the parts carefully, with sponges of gauze or cotton wetted in sterilized water or an antiseptic solution. Take the catheter out of the antiseptic solution, wash it through sterilized water, and insert it carefully without force.

Q. What should be done if there seems to be an obstruction?

Then the sister should stop at once, and send for the doctor, if the case is urgent.

Q. How should the catheter be withdrawn?

After the bladder is emptied, the catheter is withdrawn as gently as it was introduced. While removing the catheter, keep a finger over the open end, so that the few drops which it contains will not fall on the bed.

Q. What must be done after the catheter is withdrawn?

The parts are again washed as before.

Q. How should this be done?

With as little exposure as possible.

Q. What is to be done with the catheter?

It must be cleaned and laid aside.

Q. Whose duty is it to attend to the catherization?

With male patients, a man; with female patients, the nurse.

Q. May sisters assist at the operation of the bladder of a male patient?

Yes; but only then when the doctors are extremely careful.

Q. Who must dress and treat the wound after the operation?

The surgeon himself.

Q. How can the bladder be irrigated?

Should it be necessary to wash out the bladder, a long flexible tube is passed over the catheter, which is then introduced, then the ordered fluid, either warm or cold, is poured into the tube at the other end with a small pitcher, or the rubber tube is connected with an irrigator.

ENEMETA-SYRINGE AND ENEMAS.

Q. What is an enema?

It is a fluid preparation for injection into the rectum.

Q. For what purpose is it most commonly given?

To obtain an action from the bowels.

Q. What syringe is most commonly used?

One that has a rubber ball at one end or in the middle.

Q. What syringe is the best and most convenient?

A fountain syringe or irrigator, which is an enameled tin bucket or rubber bag, of different sizes, to which a rubber tube of about one and one-half yards long is attached; at its end it has a hard rubber, metal or glass nozzle attached.

Q. How can it be kept clean?

Before and after its use clean water should be passed through the syringe freely, wiped dry, and if the tube is of metal, it must be kept bright.

Q. What is to be done when an enema is to be given?

Have the ordered fluid in the basin or irrigator, the right temperature and quantity, before bringing it into the room.

Q. How should the bed be protected?

By placing a rubber and draw-sheet under the patient.

Q. What position should the patient take?

He should lie on his left side with his knees drawn up.

Q. What must be done before the tube is inserted?

Some water must be passed through the rubber tube and nozzle from the irrigator to expel the air.

Q. How is the nozzle inserted?

It must be first oiled, then, if the patient is able, he can insert the point himself, if not, then it is the duty of the nurse; if possible it should be done underneath the covers.

Q. What direction must be taken?

Toward the small of the back, and never toward the front.

Q. What might be the consequence if the wrong direction would be taken?

The intestine might be seriously injured.

Q. What should be done after the nozzle is inserted?

If it is a bulb syringe the bulb should be squeezed very slowly.

Q. What is to be done if the patient complains greatly of pain?

Rest awhile; after a delay of a few moments, you can usually go on without distress.

Q. What is to be done if the irrigator is used?

After the nozzle is inserted the irrigator must be elevated by hanging it up or holding it.

Q. What must be done if the patient is unable to bear any more?

It must be stopped at once.

Q. What should be done after an enema, if the patient has but little control?

The anus must be supported by folding a cloth and pressing it to the anus, and the patient should be kept perfectly quiet for ten or fifteen minutes.

Q. What must the sister preserve while giving an enema?

She must be quiet, careful and not hurry at all.

Q. What is frequently the reason for failure?

Because the sister does not take time enough, or the enema is not retained long enough.

Q. How long should an enema be retained?

If possible, ten to fifteen minutes.

Q. What is sometimes used in place of the nozzle?

A long, soft rubber tube about fifteen inches long.

Q. What is the enema called when this tube is used?

A high-up enema.

Q. How is this tube inserted?

It is first oiled with vaseline, then carefully inserted eight to ten inches.

Q. For what purpose are enemas given?

Either to relieve or control the bowels, or for the purpose of nourishing a patient who is not able to take the food by the mouth.

Q. What may be given for the relieving of the bowels?

From one to two pints of liquid may be used, to which sometimes either soap, salt, olive oil, castor oil, glycerine or ox-gall are added.

Q. What is generally used if the enema is given to control the bowels?

Less fluid, probably thin boiled starch mixed with cold water, and some stringent or opiate.

Q. What is taken for nourishing enema?

Various things, such as beeftea, milk and brandy, strong beef soup, beef juice and brandy, etc.

Q. How much is generally given?

Four to eight ounces; more than this might irritate and not be retained.

Q. How long must the fluid be retained?

As long as possible and no effort made to discharge.

Q. What is used for a salt enema?

One and one-half ounces of salt in one pint of warm water.

Q. What is used for an oil enema.

Either olive oil (sweet oil) or castor oil, six to eight ounces.

Q. In what cases is an oil enema often used?

After an operation of the rectum or anus, where there is likely to be a strain upon the sutures.

Q. For what is this oil injected?

In order to soften faecal mass.

Q. By what is an oil enema followed?

By an enema of water half an hour afterwards.

Q. What must be done with the oil before it is injected?

It must be warmed, for if it is cold it is too thick to pass through the syringe readily.

Q. What is used for an opium enema?

Make thin boiled starch; let it cool. Do not use more than one teaspoonful of raw starch for one enema, thin the mixture with cold water, stirring it all the time, for if it is too thick it will not pass through the tube.

Q. What is added to two ounces of this starch?

Thirty drops of laudanum, more or less, as ordered. Children require less. Ask for directions from the doctor.

Q. What is used for an oil and turpentine enema?

One-half ounce of turpentine, one and one-half ounces castor oil and three-quarters of a pint of water or soapsuds.

Q. What may be given for a nourishing enema?

Strong beeftea or beef blood squeezed from slightly broiled steak, four to six ounces; cream, one ounce; brandy as ordered by the doctor.

Q. What may be beaten together and given by rectum?

Egg and brandy, also milk and eggs.

Q. How much should be given at one time?

Not more than is likely to be absorbed, four to eight ounces; for a child from four to six ounces.

Q. What is sometimes used in obstinate cases of constipation and intestinal obstruction?

In such a case nothing proves so effective as a high-up enema, containing twelve to sixteen ounces of molasses.

Q. In what case is the daily injection of a pint of cold water often advised?

In cases where constipation is accompanied by bleeding hæmorrhoids.

Q. What is sometimes given to check a hæmorrhage from the bowels?

An injection of icewater.

Q. What enemas are given in an irritable condition of the mucous membrane?

Enemas of more soothing nature, such as thin gruel or flax-seed tea or barley water. These should always be warm.

Q. For what are anthelmintic enemas given?

To destroy worms.

Q. How much liquid is used in such a case?

A small quantity—one-half pint is sufficient for an adult; a child requires less.

Q. By whom should the remedy to be employed be prescribed?

By the physician, to suit the case.

Q. What remedies are often used?

Salt, quassia, aloes, tincture of iron, and a weak solution of carbolic acid are among those used.

Q. What are sedatives given for by an enema?
To relieve pain or quiet.

Q. How much of the medicine does it generally take?
One-third more of any drug than the dose given by mouth to produce the same effect. Ask the doctor.

Q. How must an injection for this purpose be given in order to be retained?
It must be given slowly, and the quantity should not exceed three ounces and of a temperature not exceeding 100 degrees Fahr., and the patient must be kept quiet.

Q. What syringe can be used for these small enemas?
A hard rubber syringe holding the exact quantity.

Q. What may be attached to this if the fluid should be thrown up high?
A flexible rubber tube, which may be inserted six or seven inches.

Q. Why are high-up enemas often preferred?
Because they can be given oftener and retained longer.

Q. What special care must be taken?
Not to let air come in at the time of administration of an enema.

Q. For what purpose is an enema of clear water or medicated sometimes given?
To wash out rectum and intestine when irritated.

Q. What are suppositories?
A solid body for introduction into the rectum, answering to some extent the same purpose as an enema.

Q. What size and form are they?
They vary in size, and, while they are firm enough to retain their shape under ordinary condition, they are sufficiently soft enough to melt under the heat of the body.

Q. What advantage have they?
They can be applied easier, and being small are easily retained.

Q. How should a suppository be introduced?

The suppository, having first been oiled, should be introduced very gradually and gently into the rectum, the patient lying on the left side as for an enema.

Q. How high up should the suppository be introduced?

About three inches, in order to avoid the danger of immediate expulsion.

Q. What suppositories are now frequently used?

Glycerine suppositories.

Q. What must be removed before the glycerine suppositories are inserted?

The glass tubes in which they are preserved, and it is not necessary to oil them.

Q. In what space of time do they generally produce an effect?

In fifteen to twenty minutes they produce an action from the bowels.

BEDPANS.

Q. What should be done in case the use of a bedpan is required?

Bend the knees and introduce it from the side of the bed, and, if necessary, the point may be covered with a soft cloth to absorb moisture.

Q. How can they be warmed?

By dipping them into warm water for a moment, then drying them carefully.

Q. How can the difficulty of using the bedpan, which is often felt, be overcome?

By placing the patient, if the case allows it, as much in a sitting position as possible, the back and shoulders firmly supported, keep the knees bent, and give the feet something to push against.

Q. What may be used to remove the weight of the bedclothes?

A cradle.

Q. What can be done if there is no regular fixture at hand?

Cut a barrel hoop into two half circles, cross the two pieces at right angles with each other and tie them firmly together.

Q. How is the cradle applied?

It is placed over the patient's body and the bedclothes laid over it.

Q. For what are cushions and pads used?

Various cushions and pads, which can be changed about from spot to spot as any part needs a support, are sometimes indispensible in nursing.

Q. Of what should they be made?

One or more should be made of hair, because they are cooler and firmer than feathers.

Q. With what must they be covered?

With washable goods.

MEDICINE.

Q. How may medicines be introduced into the system?

Through the mouth or skin, or mucous membrane.

Q. How many ways are there for introducing medicine through the skin?

Three different ways: in the first, the medicine is simply placed in contact with the skin, to be absorbed; in the second, rubbing or heat is applied to hasten the absorbtion; in the third, the skin is removed by blistering and the medicament sprinkled over the raw surface.

Q. Is the latter way used often?

No; it is uncertain and painful.

Q. How are medicines introduced under the skin?

By hypodermic injections.

Q. Who has to give these injections frequently?

The nursing sister and she must be thoroughly familiar with the process.

Q. What must be observed?

Several precautions. First see that the syringe is in good working order, does not leak, and then that the needle is sharp and unobstructed.

Q. How must the patient be prepared before this injection is made?

The surface where the injection is to be made, must be washed with soap and water, then with alcohol.

Q. What should be done in order to make sure that the syringe is clean?

Fill the syringe with sterilized water, adjust the needle and let the water pass through the needle, then unscrew the needle, fill the syringe about one-half full of alcohol and adjust the needle again, let the alcohol then pass through the needle.

Q. How is the medicine prepared for the injection?

If it is not already prepared in a solution, then take the tablet or powder, put it in a clean spoon or glass and add about three-fourths syringe-fulls of sterilized water and dissolve the medicine.

Q. What may hasten its dissolving?

By applying heat, by holding the spoon over a light.

Q. How is the fluid then put in the syringe?

After the needle is screwed off from the syringe, the fluid is drawn up into the syringe, then the needle adjusted.

Q. What must be done before the injection is given?

Hold the instrument with the needle upwards and force out any bubbles of air that may remain in it.

Q. How is the injection given?

Pinch up a loose fold of flesh, between the thumb and finger insert the needle quickly to the extent of an inch deeply down among the muscles, withdraw it slightly, then inject slowly the contents of the syringe.

Q. What must be done after the needle is removed?

The finger must be kept on the point of insertion for a moment, to prevent the escape of fluid.

Q. What will hasten the absorbtion?

Gentle rubbing.

Q. How must the needle be cleaned?

After using, clean the needle just as before using, by first pumping sterilized water and lastly alcohol through it, then wipe the needle and syringe dry and replace the wire in the needle at once.

Q. What does the passing of alcohol through the needle prevent?

Rusting of the needle.

Q. For what purpose are hypodermic injections given?

Either to relieve pain, or induce sleep and whenever a speedy action of a drug is important.

Q. How do remedies introduced this way act?

They act more powerfully and more rapidly than any other way.

Q. When is this injection but slightly painful?

If is skillfully performed.

Q. How can irritating fluids such as ether, brandy or camphorated oil be injected safely?

By using a clean aseptic needle and giving the injection deep in the muscles.

Q. When are such injections frequently necessary?

In a collapse (a sinking spell), after an operation.

Q. What injection is said to be the least liable to form an abcess?

Morphine.

Q. To what are abcesses due in most cases?

Either to carelessness in injecting, to the use of a syringe not thoroughly clean, or to an impure solution.

Q. Are abcesses avoidable in all cases?

No; in cases from a lowered condition of the system, which predisposes to inflammation upon slight irritation they are inavoidable.

Q. Which solutions are less irritating?

A diluted solution is less irritating than a concentrated one.

Q. What will, however, remain in some cases?
Painful spots for several days.

Q. How can they be relieved?
By bathing with alcohol or applying an ice-bag.

Q. Where should the injection be given?
Into the outer side of arm or thigh.

Q. What places must be especially avoided?
Bony prominences and inflamed parts, and caution must be observed against puncturing a vein.

Q. What has sometimes been the result from the introduction of morphine into a vein?
Death.

Q. In what condition must the medicine be, that is to be injected?
Perfectly dissolved and free from the slightest impurity.

Q. What is often added to the morphine which is to be injected?
A little atropia, one hundred and fifteenth of a grain to one fourth of a grain of morphine.

Q. For what purpose?
Because it prevents nausea and lessens the danger of poisoning.

Q. What is sometimes given to hysterical patients?
An injection of water.

Q. What is the most common way of introducing medicine into the body?
Through the mucous membrane, generally the stomach.

Q. In what form are medicines brought into the stomach?
In various forms of pills, powders, tablets and solutions.

Q. How is the trouble of swallowing pills often overcome?
By enveloping it in bread or jelly.

Q. What can be done if the patient cannot swallow them in this way?

It can be pounded up and given like powder in water, wafers, milk or syrup.

Q. How should powders be given which are insoluble in water, such as bismuth or calomel?

They may be placed dry on the tongue, and a drink of water to wash them down.

Q. How are powders given which have an objectionable taste?

Either in capsules or wafers.

Q. What is an emulsion?

A mixture of oil and water, made by rubbing with gum.

Q. What is a saturated solution?

It is a solution that contains of any substance all that can be dissolved in it.

Q. What should be done before any medicine is given?

(1) Carefully read the label before measuring the dose and again afterwards.

(2) In pouring keep the label on the upper side, to avoid defacing it.

(3) Always shake the bottle before opening it; this is often important and always harmless.

(4) Never leave the bottle longer uncorked than necessary.

Q. Where should medicines be kept?

In a dry, cool and dark closet.

Q. For what reason?

Because dampness impairs the activity of most drugs, and many are decomposed by light or heat.

Q. What is especially important in a hospital ward regarding medicine?

Never to leave dangerous drugs within reach of a patient.

Q. In what does the responsibility of a nurse consist in giving medicine?

In giving promptly, accurately and intelligently, what the doctor has prescribed.

Q. In what cases may a sister assume anything beyond this?

Only in cases of unusual emergency, and where medical advice is unattainable.

Q. What besides this should a sister try to learn about medicine?

To know the effects which the medicines she gives are intended to produce.

Q. Is it advisable to let the patient always know what he is taking?

No.

Q. What is a sister never allowed to think about the time of giving medicine?

That half an hour more or less will make no difference, or that if by accident the dose should be omitted one hour, the error could be rectified by doubling it next time.

Q. How long should the time be between medicine and food?

If no special orders are given, one half hour.

Q. How do most drugs act on an empty stomach?

Too powerfully, and some are too irritating to be borne.

Q. What medicines are always given after eating?

Arsenic, iron and cod liver oil.

Q. How is iron taken?

Through a glass tube or straw, in order to prevent injuring the teeth. If this is not done the teeth should be brushed immediately after taking it.

Q. How can cod liver oil be given?

In brandy, strong hot coffee, lemon juice or froth of beer.

Q. How should the dose be poured in the glass, spoon or cup?

In the center, so it will nowhere touch the glass, cup or spoon, and can be swallowed easily.

Q. How can medicine be given if ordered in minim doses?

If it is to be given in short intervals, then ten to twelve drops may be dropped into a glass and the same number of teaspoons of water added to it.

Q. What will this avoid?

Giving an overdose.

Q. In what case must the dose be prepared just when it is to be given?

When the medicine is volatile or evaporating.

Q. What is sometimes necessary if the patient is a child or delirious?

To give medicine by force.

Q. How can this be done?

By compressing the nostrils, so that the mouth will have to be opened for breathing.

Q. How is the medicine then given?

The medicine can be carried by a spoon far back in the mouth and emptied slowly down the throat.

Q. In what case should force be used?

If all other means fail.

Q. For what reason, only if all other means fail?

Because the excitement which it always occasions, is injurious to the patient.

LEECHES.

Q. When are leeches applied?

Leeches are commonly applied when it is desired to take a small quantity of blood from any place of the body.

Q. Where should they be applied?

Never over a large blood vessel, but over a bony surface upon which pressure can be made in case of excessive hemmorrhage.

Q. What must be done before the leeches are applied?

The part to which they are to be applied must be perfectly clean, first washed with soap and water, and again with pure water.

Q. How should the leech itself be?

Clean, and therefore to be washed and dried in the folds of a towel, before it is applied, but never handled.

Q. What will prevent the leech to bite?

Strong odors in the room, such as sulphur, vinegar or tobacco. Sometimes they even refuse to bite when the patient has taken certain drugs internally.

Q. How can a leech be induced to take hold, if he delays?

By making a slight scratch, or pricking your finger and putting a drop of blood on the place, just sufficient to give the taste of blood.

Q. How much blood will a leech take?

About one teaspoonful.

Q. In what case should the leech be held in place with a test tube or leech glass?

If applied near the eye or mouth.

Q. What can be done if the leech is applied inside the nostrils or mouth?

A thread may be put through its tail. This will not interfere with their working, and will keep them from being swallowed.

Q. How can a leech be rendered harmless, if by accident it would be swallowed?

By drinking salt water freely.

Q. How should a leech be taken off?

It should never be pulled off; if it does not drop off when it has taken sufficient blood a little salt may be sprinkled over it.

Q. What may result if they are removed by force?

The teeth of the leech will be left in the wound, where they may occasion an abscess or inflammation.

Q. How can the flow of blood be increased?

By applying hot fomentations or poultices, but the poultice must never be left on longer than a few minutes without examining it. There may be too free bleeding.

Q. How can the bleeding be checked?

By making a compress of folded squares of linen, one on top of the other, or roll up firmly some scraped lint and press it over the bites for a moment, holding it in place with the finger or strips of plaster, or a bandage; ice can also be applied.

Q. What can be done if the blood still continues to flow?

A little burnt alum can be sprinkled into the bites or they may be touched with caustic (nitrite of silver) or the doctor should be sent for.

Q. How long must a patient be watched closely after leeches have been applied?

Until all bleeding has ceased, especially at night.

CUPPING.

Q. What are cups applied for?

To relieve congestion, to abstract blood or prevent active absorption.

Q. How many kinds of cupping are there?

Two kinds; dry and wet cupping.

Q. What kind is mostly practiced for the relief of pain?

Dry cupping.

Q. What articles are needed for cupping?

Cupping glasses, spirit lamp, a saucer with alcohol, a wire with a bit of sponge or a wad of lint on the end, warm and cold water, carbolic acid, towels, a snapper and gauze.

Q. Where should the burning lamp stand?

Between the patient and the alcohol.

Q. Where should the cups be placed?

In a bowl containing warm carbolized water.

Q. How are they applied?

First wash the surface to which they should be applied, with soap and water, dry it by rubbing it with a rough towel. Dip the sponge in the alcohol, light it at the lamp and let it burn for an instant in the glass, then withdraw it, at the same time placing the cup over the afflicted part.

Q. For what reason is the flame held in the glass?

The heat will rarefy the air in it, and as it condenses on cooling a space will be left, to fill, in which the skin will be forcibly sucked up and the blood drawn toward the surface.

Q. How long are the cups left on in dry cupping?

From five to thirty minutes.

Q. What is sometimes advisable?

That instead of, as usual, allowing a cup to remain stationary, it be slid back and forth along the surface.

Q. What can be avoided by this?

The forming of circles and a large tract can be treated with one or two cups.

Q. Where should a cup never be applied?

Over a bony or irregular surface.

Q. What must be avoided above all things?

Burning the patient by using the alcohol too freely, so that it drips, or by getting the edges of the glass too hot.

Q. How can the cup be removed?

By making pressure with the finger close to it, so that the air will be admitted.

Q. What is done in wet cupping after the cup is removed?

The snapper is applied, making a series of slight cuts.

Q. What is applied then again?

The cupping cup, in the same place and in the same way as before.

Q. How can the hemorrhage be stopped after sufficient blood is extracted?

By pads of lint.

Q. What is needed on the wound?

A dry dressing or some simple ointment or oil.

Q. Where is wet cupping frequently applied?

In the lumbar region, to relieve inflammation of the kidneys.

POULTICES.

Q. What are poultices?

A gelatinous mass spread on a cloth.

Q. For what purpose are they commonly used?

For a convenient means of applying warmth and moisture.

Q. What will they often check if applied early?

The progress of inflammation and prevent the formation of pus, and when suppuration has set in, they facilitate the passage of matter to the surface and limit the spread of inflammation.

Q. For what other purpose are they applied?

For the relief of deep-seated pain.

Q. How large should a poultice be?

If applied for the relief of internal organs or to hasten maturation, it ought to be large enough to extend over a considerable surrounding surface, but over a discharging wound it should be but little larger than the opening.

Q. On what should a poultice be spread and how large should it be?

It should be spread on a stout piece of cotton, one-half to one inch thick, and not to be patted down into a hard pudding.

Q. What must be observed about the edges?

They must be as thick as the middle, or else they will dry rapidly and are painful.

Q. With what should the surface be covered?

With thin gauze or muslin, so that it will not stick to the surface, and all can be removed at the same time.

Q. What must be avoided when it is applied to the chest?

Covering the nipples

Q. How large should the cloth be on which it is spread out?

Large enough to double up all around the four sides over the edges to prevent the mass from coming out.

Q. How should the poultice be applied?

Have everything ready, the patient's clothes unfastened before you bring the poultice to the bed. Apply it immediately as warm as it can be borne.

Q. With what should it be covered?

With oil-silk, oil-muslin or rubber sheeting, and then flannel.

Q. How should it be kept?

Fastened to the place which it is intended to cover, and renewed before it is cold.

Q. How often should a poultice be changed?

This depends upon the thickness. An ordinary sized poultice will keep warm from two to three hours.

Q. When is its purpose defeated?

When it becomes a stiff, cold paste, or if it is allowed to slip about in an unsteady way.

Q. What is used whenever it is necessary to spread oil over the surface?

Vaseline.

Q. What should never be used in making a poultice?

Milk, because it becomes sour quickly and is of no value in itself.

Q. Of what are poultices made?

They are made of various materials.

Q. What makes a good simple poultice?

Several thicknesses of lint or soft cloth, wrung out in hot water and covered with a large piece of thin rubber sheeting.

Q. What is a convenient but expensive substitute for this?

Spogio-piline: this holds the heat very long.

Q. What is generally used for making a poultice?

Linseed meal.

Q. How can you make a linseed poultice?

Bring a sauce pan of water to the boiling point, and without removing it from the fire, stir into it the linseed little by little, until it has the proper consistency, just thick enough to cut with a knife. It must be smooth and free from lumps.

Q. How large can the cloth be?

Twice the size of the intended poultice; it is then spread on one half and the remainder folded back as a cover.

Q. What is sometimes omitted entirely?

A cover, and the poultice is applied directly over the skin, but portions of it are likely to adhere, so it becomes difficult to remove it neatly.

Q. What will help to keep the poultice soft?

A little oil will keep it soft and make it less likely to stick.

Q. What will help to retain the heat?

A layer of cotton or wool.

Q. In what case will this be found a valuable addition?

When the weight of a poultice is painful and in consequence thereof must be made thin.

Q. What is sometimes used for the poultice?

A flannel bag, long and free to fold over.

Q. Which is the best way to apply a large poultice for the relief of internal organs?

One or two turns of a flannel bandage about the part, and then apply the poultice in such a bag and then confine it to the place with the rest of the bandage. Arranged in this way it will keep hot a long time.

Q. What should always be used to carry the poultice to the patient?

A small board or tray.

Q. What else should be kept ready?

A basin to carry the old one away.

Q. What must be done if a new poultice is to be applied over a wound?

The old poultice being removed, the wound must be washed and protected by a piece of thin muslin or gauze wet in some disinfecting solution before the fresh one is made and applied.

Q. What other kind of poultices are sometimes prescribed?

A jacket poultice to envelope the entire chest.

Q. How is this made?

Of two pieces of muslin or other goods front and back, with strings to tie over the shoulders and under the arms.

Q. How must the edges be?

Sewed firmly, to keep the poultice from escaping.

Q. In what respect do bread poultices differ from linseed poultices?

They are lighter and more bland, but cool quickly and hold less moisture.

Q. How are they likely to become?

Not having the tenacious quality of linseed, they crumble easily and become hard and dry.

Q. How can a bread poultice be made?

Put a half a pint of boiling water over a sufficient quantity of bread crumbs, stir until a soft mass is obtained, spread about half an inch thick over a large cloth and apply.

Q. What may be added if the pain to be relieved is great?

Half an ounce of laudanum (tincture of opium).

Q. How can a slippery-elm poultice be made?

The same as a linseed poultice, using ground slippery-elm.

Q. How can a charcoal poultice be made?

Soak two ounces of bread crumbs in a half pint of boiling water; add slowly a wine glass of linseed, and when well mixed, stir in two tablespoons of powdered charcoal, mix it thoroughly and spread on a cloth. Over the surface of the poultice lastly sprinkle more charcoal.

Q. Why is bread used for a charcoal poultice?

Because it is more porous and forms a better basis.

Q. What does this poultice require?

Frequent renewal.

Q. What is this poultice used for?

For putrid sores; it absorbs the bad odor and promotes a healthy condition, but is always a dirty application.

Q. How can a bread and suet poultice be made?

By mixing equal parts of bread crumbs and mutton suet in hot water over the fire until they are thoroughly mixed.

Q. For what case is this poultice used?

It is an excellent healing poultice when the surface of the skin is broken.

Q. What makes a gentle stimulating poultice?

A yeast poultice.

Q. For what purpose is it mainly used?

To hasten the separation of gangrenous slough.

Q. How can a yeast poultice be made?

Mix a pound of ground linseed or oatmeal in a half a pint of yeast; stir gently over the fire, when warmed, spread on a cloth.

Q. In what other way can a yeast poultice be made?

Mix six ounces of yeast with the same quantity of water at blood heat; stir in fourteen ounces of wheat flour and let it stand near the fire until it rises; apply while fermenting.

Q. What else will answer for the same purpose?

Dough just as mixed for bread. It is not necessary to wait for its rises, as the heat of the body will cause it to do so. Put a sufficient quantity in a muslin bag, allowing plenty of room for it to rise.

Q. What makes a very mild poultice?

A starch poultice; it retains the heat well.

Q. What purpose is it used for?

It is used for cancers and to allay the irritation of the skin diseases.

Q. How can a starch poultice be made?

By using starch prepared as for laundry use.

Q. What poultices are thought to have a special pleasing effect?

Scraped carrots, boiled or raw.

Q. What poultices are sometimes used for their stimulating purposes?

Onions or horseradish.

Q. How can a hop poultice be made?

Fill a thin bag with hops, steep a while in hot water, wring out and apply.

Q. How can you make a bran poultice?

The same way as a hop poultice.

Q. How can a bran-jacket be made?

Cut a loose fitting jacket of cotton cloth without seams and a second one of the same shape for a lining, sew them together at the edges, leaving a small opening through which the bran can be poured in, quilt the bran here and there with large stitches to keep it in place, soak in boiling water, press it on a tray to squeeze out the excess of water.

Q. How can it be kept in place after putting it on?

With a wide roller bandage it is held close to the body.

Q. What advantage has this poultice?

It can be wet repeatedly.

Q. In what cases is it sometimes used?

In cases of pleurisy.

Q. What is sometimes added to a simple poultice?

Laudanum is sprinkled over the surface for the relief of pain.

Q. How can a spice poultice be made?

By mixing ginger, cinnamon, cloves, cayenne pepper, a teaspoonful of each, with half an ounce or more of cornmeal or flour and brandy enough to make a paste.

Q. What other form is used?

Sew the spices in a bag, stitch it several times to keep the spices in place, heat the poultice by means of dry heat and sprinkle a little whisky or brandy upon it and apply.

Q. How can you make a mustard poultice?

By adding to a simple linseed poultice a prescribed

proportion of mustard, usually from one-eighth to one-fourth (measure).

Q. What is a good substitute for a mustard poultice?

Dipping a clean, flat sponge into a mustard paste, folded in a compress and applied. The poultice may be renewed by simply moistening the sponge with warm water, its strength being perfectly preserved.

Q. How can a priessnitz poultice be made?

Take a rough towel or compress, folded three or four times, wring it out in cold water and apply, covering it with oiled silk, oiled muslin or rubber tissue.

Counter Irritants.

Q. What is the general rule in applying counter-irritants?

In applying counter-irritants do not cover a larger surface than is just necessary, and do not make them thick like a poultice.

Q. For what purpose are counter-irritants applied?

For relieving inflammation of the deeper parts.

Q. How many kinds of counter-irritants are there?

Three: (1) Such as produce merely local warmth and redness.

(2) Blistering agents.

(3) Such as produce a pustular eruption.

Q. Where are counter-irritants generally applied?

Usually over or near the seat of the disorder.

Q. Where are they sometimes applied?

At a remote part, for instance, a mustard poultice on the feet, or a mustard foot bath for the relief of the head.

Q. What is one of the most commonly used counter-irritants?

A mustard plaster or draft.

Q. How can this be made?

Take one part of powdered mustard and from two to four times the quantity of flour, according to the desired strength, mix into a paste with tepid or hot water, and spread evenly between two pieces or muslin.

Q. How long is the mustard plaster usually applied?

From twenty minutes to one-half an hour.

Q. Should a mustard plaster be left on long enough to blister?

No.

Q. Why not?

Because the sore that is produced by this is painful and slow to heal.

Q. In what case must its action be watched carefully?

If the patient is insensible or delirious, for if neglected it may cause deep ulceration.

Q. What is advisable to use for mixing, when the plaster is made for a child?

One-third of glycerine instead of pure water.

Q. For what reason?

This will render the action less severe and it can stay on longer.

Q. How can it be kept in place?

With a bandage.

Q. How can the burning sensation which follows a mustard plaster be relieved?

If it is extreme, it can be relieved by dusting the parts with flour or fine starch, or dressing it with vaseline and covering it with cotton to exclude the air.

Q. How is a cayenne pepper plaster made?

By mixing a desertspoonful of cayenne pepper in a thin paste of flour and water and spread like a mustard plaster.

Q. In what other way is red pepper sometimes applied?

A quantity of red pepper is stitched in a flat bag of flannel, wrung out in warm water, and applied over seat of pain.

Q. What mustard plasters are the most neat and quickly ready for use?

The mustard papers which are bought in the drug-store and ready for use by simply dipping them in tepid water.

Q. What is generally used to produce blistering?
Canthos or fly plaster.

Q. Where should this plaster never be applied?
Where the skin is broken, scratched or tender.

Q. How should the plaster be applied?
The part should be first washed, rubbed drp, and, if necessary, shaved?

Q. How is the plaster kept in place?
Either with adhesive strips or a bandage.

Q. What care must be taken if adhesive strips are used?
That they are not stretched tight over the canthos, or they will become painful as the blister raises.

Q. How much time is required for the blister to raise?
The time varies with different persons; for this reason examine it in three hours; it may take even four to eight hours.

Q. What is to be done in case the blister does not rise within twelve hours?
Remove the plaster and apply a poultice.

Q. How should the plaster be removed?
Carefully, so as not to tear the skin.

Q. What is to be done after the plaster is removed?
All adherent particles are cleaned off with a little oil or alcohol, and the puffed skin is snipped in at several places with sharp-pointed scissors, and the fluid will run out.

Q. What should be used for the absorption of the fluid?
Some absorbent cotton or gauze.

Q. With what is the raw surface dressed?
With vaseline, oxide of zinc or the ointment which has been ordered by the doctor.

Q. How often is this changed?
Twice a day.

Q. What is convenient for blistering an uneven surface?

Cantharial collodion, as it cannot get out of place.

Q. How is it applied?

One or two coats are applied with a camel's hair brush, and if covered with oil-silk or rubber tissue, it works more quickly.

Q. What besides this is frequently applied with a camel's hair brush?

Tincture of Iodine.

Q. What is iodine applied for?

Either for blistering or irritating the skin.

Q. What is often applied over the iodine if used for the purpose of irritating?

Glycerine and cotton.

Q. What is used to draw blisters quickly?

Strong ammonia or chloroform.

Q. How is it applied?

A piece of lint or cotton saturated with irritant is placed upon the skin.

Q. How can evaporation be prevented?

By covering it tightly with a watch-glass or the cover of a pill box.

Q. How soon will the blister be raised?

In five to ten minutes.

Q. What will this method always cause in the patient?

Pain, for the ammonia, if left too long, will eat into the flesh.

Q. How long should the canthos plaster be left on for a child?

Not more than two or four hours.

Q. When shall it be removed?

As soon as the skin is well reddened; then a bread poultice is applied to raise the blister.

Q. For what purpose?

The danger with so tender a skin is that the true skin underneath be destroyed if the plaster remains long enough to puff up the surface.

Q. How can the dressing which is to be applied after the blistering be kept in place?

With a bandage or strips of adhesive plaster.

Q. In what cases should blisters be seldom used?

In cases of aged persons or those whose circulation is poor, as they may cause extensive sores, which are slow in healing.

Q. How is croton oil applied?

Rub the surface to which the oil is to be applied with a piece of flannel; take two or three or more drops of the oil on a cloth and rub it into the surface, or apply with a feather.

Q. How often is this repeated?

At intervals of from four to six hours until small pimples appear on the spot.

Q. What must not be used after this?

No oils, nor should the burning be soothed, for irritation is wanted; a soft cloth can be tied over it to prevent the clothes from rubbing the surface.

LOTIONS.

Q. If a lotion is applied for the relieving of pain how can it be used?

Take a piece of a sheet or several folds of old linen, such as old towels or table cloths, dip in the lotion and lay it over the affected part, covering it with oil silk or rubber cloth and holding it in place with a bandage.

Q. How can the lint be re-wetted?

By squeezing a little of the lotion over it without removing it.

Q. What are evaporating lotions?

Vinegar, camphor, alcohol, etc.

Q. What are they generally mixed with and how are they applied?

They are mixed with twice the quantity of ice water and applied on a single thickness of linen.

Q. By what do they cool?

By evaporation, and therefore must be re-wetted as the cloth dries.

Q. How should they be held in place?

By a single bandage, and must not be covered with oil silk or anything else.

LINIMENTS.

Q. In what do liniments differ from lotions?

In their mode of application, being rubbed in until the part is dry.

Q. What has to be done before the liniment is applied?

The part to which the liniment is to be applied should be rubbed briskly for a few moments before.

Q. How are they applied?

A few drops are poured into the palm of the hand, then rubbed on the part with firm and even pressure until all moisture is absorbed.

Q. What must always be done after a sister has rubbed any part with liniments?

As all liniments usually contain some poisonous ingredients, the hands must be washed thoroughly before touching any sensitive spot.

OINTMENTS.

Q. How are ointments applied?

Ointments are spread on a compress, or they are rubbed in, like liniments.

Q. What is the rubbing in of ointments called?

Inunction.

APPLICATION TO THE EYE.

Q. Where and with what should a lotion be applied into the eye?

It should be introduced at the outer angle of the eye, with a glass dropper or a camel's hair brush.

Q. How can this be done?

Draw down the lower lid, and tell the patient to look up at the instant they are dropped in.

Q. What is to be done when moist clothes are ordered?

They should be laid over the eyes, but they must never be tied too fast or covered with oil silk, otherwise they will assume the nature of a poultice, which is always harmful to a delicate organ like the eye.

Q. How is the interior part of the throat treated?

By gargles or insufflation or inhalations.

Q. What are gargles?

Fluids brought in contact with the tonsils and forcibly agitated by the air from the larynx.

Q. How much should be used at a time?

A tablespoonful, four or five times successively.

Q. What must be done after an acid gargle has been used?

The mouth must be well rinsed.

Q. What is used for insufflation?

Powder, which is blown into the throat and insufflated by the patient.

Q. How can this be done?

Either with a powder blower, or the powder is placed in a glass tube, which is placed far back in the throat and blown in by the doctor or sister.

COLD APPLICATIONS.

Q. How must cold be applied?

Steadily, uniformly and over a definite space.

Q. What will render the ice bag useless or even harmful?

In case the ice bag or cold cloths slip about as the feverish patient turns and twists.

Q. How often must it be renewed?

Before it becomes warm. If this is neglected, it had better not been applied.

Q. How can a cold applicaton be made?

With an ice bag, by putting pounded ice with a little water in a thin bladder or rubber bag.

Q. How long will the water remain cold?

Until the last piece of ice is melted; before this takes place it must be renewed.

Q. What can be secured by this?

A continuous cold, and no danger from frost bite need be apprehended.

Q. Should an ice bag be filled?

No; it should only be filled about one-half, the air excluded. In this way it adapts itself better to the heated part.

Q. How should it be kept in place?

If necessary with a bandage.

Q. What is now extensively used as a substitute for ice bags?

A coil made of rubber tubing, through which ice water is syphoned from a tub or bucket placed at an elevation above the bed.

Q. To what part of the body is this mostly applied?

To the abdomen.

Q. How is it applied?

The abdomen is covered with a towel, the coil laid upon this, one end of the rubber tubing placed in the elevated bucket, the other in a bucket standing on the floor, for the water that has passed through the coil.

Q. How must the coil be started?

It must be sucked until the water commences to flow.

Q. What must be looked for?

That the elevated bucket is never empty, that nothing checks the flow of the water in the coil, that the bucket on the floor does not overflow and that the coil is kept in place.

Q. How can cold cloths be applied?

Apply single fold of linen or cotton, dipped in cold water or laid upon ice, and replace it by fresh, cool ones before it becomes warm.

Q. What does this call for?

Constant attention of the nurse.

Q. What special precaution is required?

That the bed is protected.

Q. What care must always be taken in all applications of water?

That neither the patient nor the bed clothes get wet.

Q. How can a cold drip be applied?

The easiest way for applying either a cold or warm drip or continuous drop is a can, which has a narrow pipe with a faucet attached to it and a sprinkler at the end of this pipe.

Q. Where is this placed?

On one side of the bed on a table or box, and is arranged so that the sprinkler comes just above the part afflicted. The afflicted part is then laid in a Kelley-cushion or on a rubber sheet and is covered with one or two layers of gauze and the drip turned on and regulated by the faucet. The end of the Kelley-cushion or rubber sheet is placed in a bucket aside of the bed on the floor for the drainage of the waste water.

Q. How can the drip be arranged if the above apparatus is not at hand?

Put a pitcher of water on the table higher than the patient's bed. Put one end of a long strip of lint or lampwick in the pitcher, lay the other across the dressings which are applied to the inflamed part.

Q. What care must be taken?

That the waste water is conveyed into a basin or bucket, and not allowed to soak in the bed.

HOT APPLICATIONS AND FOMENTATIONS.

Q. What are fomentations?

They are poultices in modified forms, applications of hot water, pure or medicated, by means of pieces of flannel or flat sponges.

Q. What advantage have they?

They are clean, light and quickly prepared.

Q. What do they require?

Constant attention, needing to be changed every ten to fifteen minutes.

Q. What are stupes?

Pieces of flannel doubled to the desired size; these are to be saturated with boiling water and wrung out as dry as possible.

Q. What is needed for this purpose?

A stupe wringer.

Q. How can this be made?

Take a piece of toweling with a wide hem at each end and a stick run through the hem at each end.

Q. How can this wringer be used?

Put the stupe in the middle, saturate with boiling water, and twist the sticks in opposite directions until no more water can be squeezed out.

Q. When is a stupe of little use?

If it is cool enough to be wrung out with the hands.

Q. What may be used in place of a stupe wringer?

A towel, but there is danger of scalding the fingers.

Q. How dry should the stupe be?

Dry enough not to wet the bed or the clothing.

Q. How many layers of flannel should be used?

Two or more.

Q. How is it applied?

Have everything ready, shake the flannel slightly after taking it out of the towel.

Q. For what reason should the flannel be shaken?

To let the air in between the layers, and they will keep hot longer.

Q. With what should the stupe be covered?

With oil silk or oiled muslin, an inch larger in each direction, and over that lay a piece of dry flannel or a layer of cotton.

Q. How should the stupe be kept?

Always warm and never allowed to get cold.

Q. What must be done after the fomentations are discontinued?

The part to which they have been applied must be carefully dried and covered for a time with a warm dry flannel.

Q. To what are fomentations never applied?

To a discharging wound.

Q. For what reason?

Because the stupes would be soiled at once.

Q. What are they chiefly used for?

For the relief of spasm of the internal organs.

Q. What is turpentine liable to do when sprinkled on a stupe?

It will easily blister.

Q. What precautions must be taken?

The sore spots must be covered with some dressing.

Q. What is employed to avoid the relaxation of tissues?

DRY FOMENTATIONS.

Q. How can they be made?

By heating thin bags of sand, ashes, salt, bran, hops, hot bricks, plates, tins, water bottles, etc.

Q. What must be done before these fomentations are applied?

They must be wrapped up or covered.

Q. For what purpose?

Because there is danger that the patient might be burned.

Q. When is this especially necessary?

With a child or an unconscious patient.

Q. What has often happened where this precaution was neglected?

That patients after operations before recovering from the anæsthetic suffered severe burns.

Q. Who is to be blamed for such an occurrence?

A carelessness on the part of the nurse, which is simply unpardonable.

Q. What applications are generally best?
Hot applications are generally better than cold ones.

Q. What are cold applications chiefly used for?
To subdue inflammation.

Q. When are cold applications never used?
When pus is forming or during sloughing.

BATHS.

Q. What is very important for preserving health and promoting recovery from disease?
Daily bathing.

Q. Why?
Because all vital organs are affected through the skin.

Q. What benefit is derived by keeping the skin in clean, healthy condition?
The circulation of the blood, the action of the kidneys and bowels, and all the digestive processes are promoted, many diseases warded, and the assimilation of food aided.

Q. Whom shall the sister ask for directions in regard to the bathing of a patient?
The doctor; not only what kind of a bath to give, but also at what degree of temperature.

Q. What is often the consequence of ignorance in this matter?
Great harm to the patient.

Q. At what temperature are baths given?
Cold at 50 to 60 Fahr.
Temperate at 75 to 85 Fahr.
Tepid at 85 to 96 Fahr.
Warm at 96 to 98 Fahr.
Hot at 98 to 110 Fahr.

Q. How can you prepare a bran bath?
Boil a pound of bran in a bag for a quarter of an hour, drain off the fluid, and add water to the fluid.

The Nursing Sister.

Q. Is there any other way?

Put enough bran in cold or warm water to make the water milky.

Q. Is it advisable to give this latter bath in a stationary bath tub?

Never; for in letting off the water, the bran will be sucked down and will give choke to the pipes.

Q. For what purpose is this bath chiefly given?

For softening the skin when it is dry and flaky.

Q. How can a salt bath be given?

Take one pound of rock salt to four gallons of water.

Q. Must the salt be increased?

Yes; in proportion to the quantity of water.

Q. What must be done after the bath?

The body must be rubbed briskly.

Q. In what case is this especially useful?

To invigorate feeble constitutions.

Q. When given daily cold, as a sponge bath, what are the effects?

It lessens the susceptibility to cold, rheumatism, etc.

Q. How is a sulphur bath prepared?

By adding to each gallon of water twenty grains of sulphurate of potasssium.

Q. In what must this be prepared and given?

In a wooden or porcelain lined vessel.

Q. For what reason in a porcelain lined vessel?

Because the sulphates discolor most metals.

Q. What is it used for?

For skin diseases or rheumatism.

Q. What kind of water should be used for all baths of skin diseases?

Rain water or softened water.

Q. What should be done after the bath?

The skin should not be rubbed, but dapped dry with soft towels.

Q. How can you prepare a soda bath?

By adding one pound of common baking soda to the bath.

Q. For what is it used?

For the same purpose as the sulphur bath.

Q. What should be done first with the soda?

It should be dissolved in warm water, after which water of any temperature may be added in a sufficient quantity for a plunge bath.

Q. How can you prepare a starch bath?

By mixing half a pound of starch with two quarts of water, to be added to the bath.

COLD DOUCHE.

Q. In what cases is a cold douche sometimes ordered?

In cases of inflammation of the brain, and to subdue delirium in fever.

Q. What must be done if the hair is very thick?

It should be shaved or cut off very close.

Q. How is a patient to be prepared for this douche?

Raise the patient in the bed and bend his head forward over an empty basin.

Q. How can you protect his shoulders?

By laying a piece of oil-silk or a rubber sheet between several folds of soft towels around his shoulders.

Q. Where is the water then poured?

The cold water is poured over the crown of the head into an empty basin.

Q. How is the water poured?

The pitcher being slowly and gradually raised higher and higher, so that the water may fall with more force.

Q. How is the head then dried?

The head is dried without rubbing.

HOT PLUNGE BATH.

Q. In what cases are hot plunge baths frequently given?

In cases of eruptive fevers.

Q. How is the patient lifted into the bath?

Wrap him up in a sheet or bathing apron, and put him, sheet and all, into the water for ten or fifteen minutes.

Q. Against what is the patient to be protected?
Against all exposure.

Q. What must be warmed afterwards?
Towels, night clothes and bedding.

Q. What will a very hot bath do?
It excites and stimulates the nervous system.

Q. What may be the consequence, if the water it too hot or the bath is continued too long?
Languor, giddiness or faintness.

Q. With what should the temperature of the water be tested?
With a thermometer, and the same degree of heat kept up throughout.

Q. What special care must be taken?
That no part of the body comes directly under the hot water tap.

Q. How should the head of the patient be kept?
Cool.

Q. For what purpose is a hot foot bath generally given?
To relieve the head and to promote perspiration.

Q. How hot should it be given?
Hot enough to make the skin decidedly red, and more hot water should be added from time to time.

Q. How far up should the water reach?
Up to the knees.

Q. What must be covered?
The patient and the tub should be covered with a blanket.

Q. What can be added to the water if greater relief of the head is required?
Mustard: about half a teaspoonful to a pail of water.

Q. How long should the bath last?
From fifteen to thirty minutes.

Q. What should be used in bed after the bath?

Warm stockings or a small blanket to protect the limbs.

Sponge Bath.

Q. What special care must be taken when a sponge bath is to be given in bed?

The chief things are that: 1. The bed be protected with a rubber sheet and a draw sheet. 2. That the patient's arms are slipped out of the sleeves. 3. That a dry night shirt is always put on after the bath.

Q. How much water should be taken up?

As little as possible, but return the cloth to the water frequently.

Q. How often should the water be changed?

Two or three times during the bath.

Q. What should stand at the side of the bed?

A slop jar or pail for the dirty water.

Q. What must be on hand before the bath is begun.

Everything that is needed.

Q. How should the patient be washed and dried?

Only one part at a time.

Q. How should the patient be dried?

With soft towels in quick, gentle strokes.

Q. What should be done with the part as soon as it is washed?

It should be enveloped in a towel.

Q. What will this avoid?

Exposure.

Vapor Bath.

Q. How can you give a vapor bath in a simple way?

Undress the patient, put a thin flannel or woolen cloth about him, seat him on an arm-chair, place by his side a pail of boiling water, into which, as it cools, you put bricks made very hot, and cover the patient, chair and pail with a large blanket, fastened securely at the neck.

Q. What will the steam soon produce?

The required perspiration.

Q. What care will be necessary?

That the bed, bedclothes, towels and night-shirts are made hot before the patient uses any of them.

Q. What other bath can be given in the same manner?

A hot air bath with a spirit lamp.

Q. What precautions must be taken when using a lamp?

Against fire.

Q. What is used frequently for a hot air bath?

A special apparatus which is heated by a spirit lamp or a gas burner.

Q. What is required if the vapor or hot air bath is to be given in bed?

A cradle.

Q. How can the hot air bath or vapor bath be given in bed?

Remove the sheets and take off the patient's clothes; put blankets next to the patient and over the cradle so as to render it almost air-tight.

Q. How can it be arranged so that the vapor can enter under the bedclothes.

A gas stove or spirit lamp is placed on a chair close to the bed: a croup-kettle which has a large nozzle is useful for this purpose; this is placed on the lamp and the nose of the kettle is introduced under the bedclothing.

Q. What may be done when the perspiration is established freely?

The patient may be rubbed with warmed towels, and warmed cloths put on.

Q. What must be put on the bed?

Dry warm sheets and blankets, but without exposing or disturbing the patient.

Q. How is a hip bath given?

The patient is immersed, the knees to the waist, and covered with a blanket.

Q. How should the temperature of the water be kept?

It should be kept as ordered by the doctor, either warm or cold.

Q. How long should this bath be prolonged?

About twenty minutes.

Q. What is generally the purpose of this bath?

To excite the menstrual flow.

Q. At what time should the bath be given?

As nearly as can be calculated at the time when that would appear.

Q. What is sometimes employed for the same purpose?

A hot foot bath.

COLD PLUNGE OR PACK.

Q. What are cold baths employed for?

Either to produce reaction, refrigeration or a nervous shock.

Q. What does cold water do?

It abstracts the heat from the body and affects the internal organs through the nervous system.

Q. What is first experienced upon entering a cold bath?

A sense of chilliness and depression.

Q. How does it affect the pulse and temperature?

The pulse is quickened, but the temperature of the surface is lowered and the blood accumulates in the internal organs.

Q. What will soon follow this condition?

A reaction, with invigorated circulation, and a feeling of warmth.

Q. What will return if the bath is continued too long?

The coldness returns, with weakness of pulse and general depression.

Q. When should a cold bath not be given?

When a patient feels chilly, although his bodily temperature is high, or when there is free perspiration, when the patient feels faint or during menstruation.

Q. What must be done if shivering comes on during the bath?

The patient should at once be taken out of the bath and put to bed, heat applied and stimulants given if it persists.

Q. For what are cold baths sometimes given?

They are sometimes used as a tonic in cases of debility.

Q. At what time is it best given?

In the morning, and followed by vigorous rubbing and gentle exercise.

Q. For what purpose is it mostly given?

To bring down speedily a high temperature.

Q. How can it be given?

The patient is undressed, rolled in a sheet, and put in an empty tub or fever cot and buckets of cold water poured over the body for two or three minutes until he is evidently cool.

Q. What is done after the water is poured over the body the prescribed length of time?

The patient is then rolled in a dry sheet and put back to bed, without any exertion on his part, and covered with blankets.

Q. Who should be present at the first bath, if possible?

The doctor.

Q. What should be done if he has gone and unforeseen symptoms appear?

The bath should be postponed until further instruction.

Q. What can be done if the patient is not able to stand the shock of cold water poured over him?

Then the patient is laid in a tub half filled with water at 95 to 98 degrees and gradually cooled down to 80 or 60 degrees, as ordered, with ice or cold water.

Q. What should the sister do during the bath?
She should rub the patient in the water.

Q. What is a fever cot?
It is a wooden frame, covered with sacking, below which a rubber sheet is hung, one end lower than the other.

Q. How must the bed be prepared if a cold pack is to be applied?
A large rubber sheet must be first spread upon the bed, then two or three blankets.

Q. What is spread over the blankets?
A sheet wrung out in cold water.

Q. Where is the patient placed?
The patient, who has been stripped of his clothes, is then laid upon this wet sheet and it is folded over him, tucked in well at both sides.

Q. What should not be included in the sheet?
The ankles and feet.

Q. What should be done with the blankets?
They should be folded one by one over the patient.

Q. How long should the patient be left in this pack?
From fifteen to twenty minutes or longer if ordered.

Q. What should be given to the patient while in the pack?
Plenty to drink.

Q. How must the feet be kept?
Warm.

Q. What effect will this generally have upon the patient?
It will render the skin moist, subdue restlessness and delirium and reduce fever.

Q. What should be done when the pack is removed?
Dry off the patient quickly and wrap him in a dry, warm blanket for some hours.

Q. How can a cold pack be given if its object is only to reduce fever?
By spreading a rubber cloth over the bed, then wrap-

ping the patient in sheets which have been wrung out in cold water without using the blankets.

Q. What is generally used then?

Friction, by rubbing the different parts of the body while the patient is wrapped, and water sprinkled over him.

Q. How can the same effect be produced easier?

By applying towels wrung out in ice water, dry enough not to drip, one after another, from the neck downward.

Q. What is to be done when the feet are reached?

Begin again at the head and renew each in succession.

Q. How long should this be continued?

As long as necessary to reduce the temperature or as prescribed by the doctor.

Q. What besides this is given to relieve a feverish condition?

A cold or tepid sponge bath.

Q. How can it be given?

If possible, strip the patient, lay him between blankets and sponge freely under the covers.

Q. What should be applied while giving a cold sponge bath?

A cold compress or icebag to the head and a hot-water bottle to the feet.

Q. How should the sponging always be done?

Downward.

Q. What should be done after the bath?

The patient should be left undisturbed in the blanket for at least ten to fifteen minutes.

Q. What is often added to the water?

Alcohol.

Q. For what purpose?

This makes it more cooling by its rapid evaporation.

MASSAGE.

Q. What is massage?

It is a peculiar rubbing and kneading of the underlying muscles.

Q. What will answer when friction is needed to excite circulation of the blood?

Brisk rubbing up and down with the bare hand or a hair glove all over the surface of the body.

Q. Which is the best time for this?

In the morning before dressing, after the patient's bath.

Q. What should be done if there is stiffness and inaction of the muscles?

The entire body should be treated by pinching and rubbing the muscles and tendons.

Q. With what should this be done?

With the whole hand and not with the fingers alone.

Q. What should be done with each joint?

It should be worked up and down and backward and forward.

Q. How is this done?

Evenly and without jerking, commencing at the toes and going upwards.

Q. What is frequently used for rubbing?

Cocoa oil or vaseline.

Q. How should the rubbing be done when restless, nervousness or fatigue is to be overcome?

It should be done in one direction, in long, slow, firm strokes.

Q. Where should you begin?

With the shoulders and arms, then the back, abdomen, thighs, legs and feet.

Q. What effect will this have?

It soothes and induces sleep.

Q. How long is a patient generally rubbed?

From one-half to one hour.

Q. What should be avoided as much as possible?
Exposure.

SOME SPECIAL MEDICAL CASES.

Q. What may be called the general causes of many diseases?

Proximity to stagnant water, exhalation from defective drain, sewers and cess-pools, damp cellars, impurities in drinking water, sudden changes from heated rooms to damp night air, mental or bodily over fatigue, insufficient clothing and food, etc.

Q. What, therefore, should be done in cases of serious illness or long continued ill-feeling?

The cause should be looked for and a remedy or preventative applied.

Q. What persons will be liable to take the same diseases?

Persons living under the same condition.

Q. What is therefore of great importance?

The early stages of any disease.

Q. What should excite attention?

A loss of appetite, a feeling of general lassitude, flushing of the face and wandering pain in the back and limbs, sore throat, sleeplessness, in short, anything unusual in the appearance or feeling.

Q. What may the neglect of these seeming trifles make?

The difference between an unimportant indisposition and a serious illness.

Q. What is, therefore, to be done upon the first appearance of such symptoms?

It is well to enforce rest, a long morning sleep, followed by a tepid sponge bath and some light nourishment before dressing for the day.

Q. What food should be taken?

The simplest food and not much of it.

Q. What should be avoided and what should be secured?

No exercise should be taken, but as much fresh air as

8—

possible by day and by night should be secured, and in all cases the patient should occupy a bed alone.

Q. What can generally be given safe?

Two grains of quinine in twelve hours.

Q. With what should the bowels be regulated if constipated?

With a plain enema of warm soapsuds.

TYPHOID FEVER.

Q. Which is the principal characteristic of typhoid fever?

Ulceration of the bowels.

Q. How long may premonitory symptoms precede the disease?

For days and even weeks.

Q. Which are such symptoms?

Restless sleep, mental disquietude, dizziness, pain in the different parts of the body, hot dry skin, and slight nosebleed, sometimes nausea, slight diarrhœa, and a general ill-feeling.

Q. How does the fever generally announce itself?

With a chill or a long continued chilly sensation, and the bodily temperature rises.

Q. What must be done on the part of the nurse?

She must follow with utmost exactness the orders of the doctor.

Q. How long is the general duration of the disease?

Three to four weeks, dating from the first rise of temperature.

Q. What symptoms usually appear the first week?

A general increase of temperature, though it may have a remittent type, falling in the morning but rising every night a little higher, till it gets up to 103 to 104 degrees.

Q. What other symptoms will generally appear by this time?

Violent headache, intolerance of light, and perhaps, slight delirium, parched lips and tongue, abdominal tenderness and tympanites.

Q. What are the symptoms usually in the second week?

During the second week the temperature remains continuously high and an eruption of rose-colored spots may appear on the abdomen and chest.

Q. How are these spots?

They are slightly elevated and disappear upon pressure, to return again immediately.

Q. How long does each spot remain visible?

Three days.

Q. How are head and bowels generally by this time?

The headache is less, the bowels are likely to be relaxed, the movements of a light ochre or pea-soup color.

Q. What does the patient assume in severe cases?

A characteristic typhoid appearance, the face dusky and indifferent, the muscular prostration evidently extreme, the mental condition one of a stupor, varied by active dilirium.

Q. How is the tongue?

Brown and dry and heavily coated; sordes collect on the teeth.

Q. How is the fever during the third week?

The fever again becomes remittent, falling towards morning, though rising at night.

Q. How is the general typhoid condition at this period?

It deepens, the pulse becomes frequent and feeble, and rapid loss of strength.

Q. What period is the third week generally in typhoid?

The period of greatest danger.

Q. What should appear at the beginning of the fourth week?

Evident improvement, the fever becoming intermittent, and the evening temperature decreasing, the tongue clearing off, the tympanites disappearing.

Q. What is of the greatest importance in typhoid fever?

Good nursing.

Q. What must a sister therefore do?

She must keep a constant watchfulness and care from the beginning until complete recovery.

Q. In what position must the patient be kept?

In a recumbent—that is a lying-down posture.

Q. How long must this posture be maintained?

Until the intestinal ulcers are completely healed.

Q. What must a sister observe in typhoid fever?

The symptoms, viz: Whether the patient talks in his sleep; is clear-headed when spoken to, but listless; has great thirst; a bitter taste in the mouth; a sore tongue; whether there is any rash on the abdomen, or whether the abdomen is puffed up.

Q. What must be very exactly observed?

The character of the secretions, quantity, color, quality.

Q. How often should the temperature be taken?

As often as ordered by the doctor, which is usually every four hours, should be recorded immediately, the rapidity and evenness of the pulse and respirations at the corresponding time.

Q. What does labored breathing, especially in sleep, often indicate?

An inflammation of the air-passages.

Q. What does frequently occur during convalescence?

A relapse; usually in a milder form than the original attack and of shorter duration.

Q. What is the greatest danger in typhoid fever?

A perforation of the bowels by the intestinal ulcers and consequently acute peritonitis.

Q. What are the symptons of perforation?

Severe pain, increased by pressure, rapid distention of the abdomen, rapid, feeble pulse and other signs of collapse.

Q. In how many hours is it usually fatal?

In twenty-four hours.

Q. From what may intestinal hemorrhage occur?

It may occur without perforation from the rupture of an artery in some ulcer.

Q. By what is a rupture generally preceded?

By a sudden fall of temperature.

Q. In what does the treatment consist after a hemorrhage?

In absolute rest and the application of an ice-bag or ice-coil over the abdomen.

Q. At what temperature should the room be kept?

At 65 degrees in winter.

Q. How should the room be ventilated?

With an open window and an open fire-place, if possible. Let no draught blow upon the patient, but keep the air constantly changing.

Q. For what reason is this so absolutely necessary?

Because the atmosphere is filled with poisonous influences and germs from the disease.

Q. Where do these come from?

From the skin, the breath, and the secretions of the patient.

Q. How can this poison be removed?

By free currents of fresh air through the room, but never over the patient.

Q. With what should the bed be protected?

It should be protected with a rubber sheet and a draw sheet.

Q. With what should the patient be covered?

With the top sheet and a blanket if necessary, but no quilts.

Q. Should warm covers be used to keep up a free perspiration?

No.

Q. What is desirable?

A moist skin.

Q. How can this be promoted?

It is more likely to be promoted by cool bathing than by warm bedclothes.

Q. On what should a fever patient never be laid?

On a feather bed.

Q. What pillow should be used?

If it can be secured, a small, rather hard pillow is the best.

Q. For what reason?

Because, with a large, easily compressed feather pillow the head is kept too warm, and sinking into it the air is kept out from the lungs.

Q. How should the pillows be arranged?

In such a way that the chest is expanded, the shoulders being supported.

Q. How often should the entire body be sponged?

As often as ordered by the doctor, which is generally every two hours when having high temperature, with cold or warm water, as ordered, and, if ordered, adding about one ounce of alcohol to a basin half full of water.

Q. What must be washed carefully?

All the creases in the skin, particularly those parts which are soiled by the excretions.

Q. What will be the consequence if this is neglected for awhile?

It cannot be made good by after-care: bed sores are apt to form, where there is no absolute cleanliness.

Q. What must be done on account of the frequent involuntary passages from the bowels?

A careful watch must be kept both of the person and clothing, that everything may be kept clean and dry.

Q. What precautions must be taken after the body, bed and clothing are cleaned?

Precautions to keep them so.

Q. What should be used for this reason?

A draw sheet across the bed. They are easily removed and changed without exhausting the patient's strength.

Q. What can be done besides the general sponging?

The face and hands should be sponged repeatedly during the day. A small piece of ice can be put in a sponge and passed across the forehead now and then.

Q. What can be laid across the temples?

A soft, thin cloth folded once and dipped in some evaporating lotion, like alcohol and water, which must be changed before it becomes warm.

Q. For what purpose does this serve?

For a double purpose; it is cleanly and has a tendency to lower the fever which consumes the patient's strength.

Q. What will form across the lips and teeth in neglected cases of fever?

A black crust.

Q. How can this be prevented?

By washing the mouth, teeth and tongue with cool water or a mouth-wash and a soft rag.

Q. What can be used if the skin is broken?

Add to a tumbler of water a teaspoonful of chlorate of potash or borax.

Q. What will answer the purpose if the skin is not broken?

Salt water or a slice of lemon rubbed across the teeth and about the mouth.

Care of the Room.

Q. What care must be taken besides the attention given to the patient and bed?

That the room and the furniture are scrupulously clean; no soiled towels, napkins or other articles must be allowed hanging about.

Q. What should be kept in the bed-pans or vessels?

Two or three ounces of carbolized water or some other disinfectant.

Q. What must be done as soon as they are removed from the bed?

A clean cloth must be thrown over them, covering the handle and all.

Q. What will this prevent?

This prevents the air of the room from being contaminated and the nurse from breathing poisonous exhalations.

Q. By what is typhoid fever more readily conveyed?

By these exhalations, more so than in any other way.

Q. How often should the night-clothes be changed?

Night and morning; the sheets twice or more.

Q. What may be done for the patient's comfort?

If his strength permits and a second bed can be had, he may be lifted into a fresh bed for the night, while the warm and damp mattress in use all day should be carried out and aired.

Q. May a typhoid patient get up out of bed?

Never allow the patient to get up, not even the first week.

Q. What should be used to avoid exertion?

Bedpan and urinal.

Q. To what is a fever patient disposed?

To slide down from the pillows and to lie in the same position all the time.

Q. What must a sister do to prevent this?

She must keep a close watch against this, keep him well on the pillows, turn him from one side to another, putting a pillow snug to his back to support him.

Q. For what reason are these changes so necessary?

Because long lying in one position will make the spot on which pressure comes tender, and bed sores may form.

Q. What must be examined every day?

The back, hips and heels, and if any redness occurs, bathe the place four times a day with diluted alcohol or some other solution, dust with powder and use air-cushions.

Q. Whose directions must be followed in giving medicine?

The doctor's.

Q. What must be reported?

Any change of symptoms observed following the dose and the same with stimulants.

Q. What will sometimes be needed in feeding the patient?

All the ingenuity of the nurse to make the patient take the milk, beef tea, etc.

Q. How is beef tea generally more readily taken?

Cold, and when there is a tendency for diarrhœa it should never be given warm.

Q. What is sometimes given in extreme cases?

Beef tea of the strongest kind and milk punch alternately at intervals of an hour, half-hour or less, as the doctor directs.

Q. What should a sister never do when brandy or wine are ordered?

She should never follow her own judgment as to the quantity, but should request the doctor to say how much of either he wishes to be given in twenty-four hours.

Q. How can it be given?

It can either be given as a cool drink with ice water, or in milk, in broken doses during the specified time.

Q. In what case is a sister justified to give the patient on her own responsibility a tablespoon of brandy in hot water?

In case of faintness, or exhaustion after purging, or a chilly sensation that cannot be relieved by extra blankets or hot bottles.

Q. How much cold water may be given with safety?

If the physician has no objection, as much cold water can be given as the patient wants, but it must have been previously boiled and cooled.

Q. What is this needed for?

It is needed to supply the waste through perspiration.

Q. By what may cold water be substituted if there is trouble with the bowels?

By arrow root, or barley, or toast water iced.

Q. What must be given to patients who are too ill to ask for a drink?

Cooling drinks must be given them frequently in a feeding-cup.

Q. What should a sister never miss regarding this?
Never let the patient go without them.

Q. What is refreshing to the patient?
Small bits of ice, but they do not take the place of water.

Q. What is the sister to do if the patient is delirious?
Never leave the patient alone; never contradict what he may say; accompany him to the moon if he wishes it.

Q. How should she never speak to him?
Never loud; he is not deaf because he is delirious.

Q. How can he be kept in bed?
If there is no other way, lay a long, folded draw sheet across the blanket and tuck it well under the mattress on either side.

Q. Is a delirium always alarming?
A light delirium need not to excite alarm, unless it is of the low muttering kind, accompanied with pulling at the bed clothes or reaching up into the air after some imaginary object.

Q. What is to be dreaded?
Confusion of thoughts, loss of recollection of recent events, anxious look or a wandering and vacant eye.

Q. What are some of the dangers of the fever?
Internal hemorrhage, diarrhœa, perforation of the bowels and pneumonia.

Q. What may sometimes occur during the second week or later?
Death may occur simply from incaution on the part of the nurse in permitting the patient to sit up or make some seeming harmless exertion, or to eat harmless food in too large quantities.

Q. What may not be indulged in convalescence?
The patient's appetite.

Q. What kind of food may be given?
Nourishing food in small quantities, frequently, once in two hours, if necessary.

Q. When may solid food be given?

Not until distinctly permitted by the doctor.

Q. What is one of the accompaniments of typhoid fever?

Dyspepsia, hence more food than can be assimilated at one time is very dangerous.

Q. What must at once be reported to the doctor?

A moderate indigestion, a trifling diarrhœa, a slight nausea.

Q. For what reason are they so dangerous?

Because any violent straining may induce perforation of the bowels at points of ulceration.

Q. What must be advanced before going outdoors is permitted?

The strength must be considerably advanced, but fresh air should be procured as much as possible.

Q. What are the life saving agents in typhoid fever?

Careful nursing and diet regulation.

Q. What does undiluted milk do upon entering the stomach?

It becomes almost solid.

Q. Why should stools be carefully examined?

To see whether there are any curds of milk in it.

Q. How much milk is given for exclusive milk diet?

One to three quarts in twenty-four hours.

Q. How are natural milk stools?

They are not too hard, without coagular of casein or flakes of fat.

Q. What indicates that milk is well digested?

A clean tongue and a soft abdomen.

Q. What does the reverse of these symptoms suggest?

That the milk is supplied in too large a quantity or that it is not being digested.

Q. What must therefore be done?

Three things: 1. The quantity must be reduced. 2. The mode of administration must be changed. 3. The milk must be prepared or pre-digested.

Q. How much milk is believed to be sufficient?

Four ounces given every two to three hours.

The following list may serve as a guide when the patient is first permitted to take solid food:

First Day—Chicken broth, thickened with thoroughly boiled rice; milk toast or cream once a day.

Second Day—Junket, mutton broth and bread crumbs, with toast, a tender piece of beefsteak may be chewed but not swallowed.

Third Day—A small scraped beef sandwich, tender sweetbread, bread and milk, a soft cooked egg or baked apple for supper.

Fourth Day—The soft part of two or three oysters, meat broth, thickened with a beaten egg, cream toast, rice pudding or blancmange and whipped cream.

Fifth Day—Scraped beef sandwich, tender sweetbread, bread and milk, a poached egg, gelatine.

Sixth Day—Mush and milk, scrambled egg, chicken jelly, bread and butter.

Seventh Day—Small piece of tenderloin steak or a little breast of boiled chicken, bread and butter, boiled rice, wine jelly, sponge cake and whipped cream.

Eighth Day—A slice of rare tender roast beef, a thoroughly baked mealy potato, served with butter or mashed with cream.

Ninth Day—A little broiled fresh fish for breakfast, beefsteak at dinner, rice, macaroni, eggs, sago, rice or milk pudding, a baked apple.

Tenth Day—Mush and milk, a squab or breast of a partridge or roast chicken, other food as before.

For the next four or five days the patient may select articles from the previous days, so that three good meals are taken a day, besides three or four glasses of milk taken between meals.

The following diet list will serve as a general guide

for feeding convalescents from fevers of ordinary severity in which special lessons of the alimentary canal are not present:

First Day.

Breakfast—Poached egg on toast, cocoa.

Lunch—Milk punch.

Dinner—Raw oysters, cream crackers, and if desired, light wine.

Lunch—Cup of hot broth.

Supper—Milk toast, wine jelly and tea.

Second Day.

Breakfast—Soft cooked egg, milk punch, coffee with sugar and cream.

Lunch—Cup of soft custard.

Dinner—Strained soup, sippets of toast, a little barley pudding with cream, sherry wine if desired.

Lunch—Milk punch.

Supper—Water toast, buttered, wine jelly, tea.

Third Day.

Breakfast—Scrambled egg, cream toast, cocoa.

Lunch—Cup of hot chicken broth.

Dinner—Chicken or broiled steak, bread, light wine and a little tapioca pudding.

Lunch—An eggnogg.

Supper—Buttered dry toast, baked apple and cream, tea.

Fourth Day.

Breakfast—An orange, oatmeal with cream and sugar, poached egg on toast, baked potato, cocoa.

Lunch—Cup of soft custard.

Dinner—Soup, a small piece of beefsteak, creamed potatoes, baked custard, coffee.

Lunch—One cup of chicken broth with rice.

Supper—Raw oysters, crackers, graham bread toasted, wine jelly, tea.

FIFTH DAY.

Breakfast—An orange, coffee, oatmeal with cream and sugar, broiled mutton-chop, toast.

Lunch—One cup of mulled wine.

Dinner—Chicken soup, bread, creamed sweetbreads, baked potato, snow pudding, cocoa.

Lunch—An eggnogg.

Supper—Buttered dry toast, orange jelly, sponge cake and cream tea.

TYPHUS.

Q. What is typhus fever?

It only resembles typhoid by name; it is a highly contagious disease, associated with overcrowding and bad ventilation.

Q. How does the attack usually begin?

With a chill, followed by a temperature of 105 degrees or more, with violent headache and extreme prostration.

Q. When does the rash appear?

Toward the end of the first week, showing on the sides of the abdomen, dirty pink or purplish spots.

Q. How is the rash called when abundant?

Mulberry rash.

Q. How long does each spot persist?

Until the disease terminates in convalescence or death.

Q. What is especially affected?

The head; violent delirium will occur.

Q. How does the disease run?

Usually fourteen days, after which the amendment will be abrupt, as the onset was.

Q. What must be saved in every possible way?

The patient's strength, the aim being to sustain the vital powers until the fever abates.

Q. What other precautions should be kept up?

Constant watch during the delirium; keep ice-bag on the head, sleeplessness must be relieved, and nourishment must be given, if by force.

Q. What is especially important?

Ventilation, because much poison is thrown off from lungs and skin.

SCARLET FEVER OR SCARLETINA.

Q. How does scarlet fever usually begin?

With headache, nausea, sore throat, pains in limbs, rapid pulse and a rise of temperature of 100 to 104 or 105 degrees.

Q. At what time does the rash appear?

Generally the second day, beginning at the neck and chest and extending over the whole body.

Q. Where is it the deepest?.

On the neck, the back, the outer side of the limbs, the joints, hands and feet.

Q. Of what color are the cheeks?

A bright deep red.

Q. What must be done as soon as the case has been declared for scarlet fever?

The patient must be insolated, all precautions given for infectious diseases should be observed, and every order of the physician carried out faithfully.

Q. At what temperature should the room be kept?

An even temperature of 65 degrees; if possible, a light fire, and leave the window down an inch at the top.

Q. How and how often should the room be ventilated thoroughly?

Twice a day; the windows should be thrown open wide and the air entirely changed.

Q. What must be done with the patient during this time?

The patient must be covered head and all until the room is again warm.

Q. How often should the patient be sponged or bathed?

Two or three times a day with warm water as directed.

Q. What care must be taken?

That he be covered with a blanket during the bathing.

Q. What should be done after the bath?

The patient should be dried quickly with warm, soft towels, without rubbing, and as the patient lies in bed rub the entire surface of the body with vaseline or whatever oil the physician orders.

Q. How should the bed-clothing be?

It should be warm but never heavy. Keep the feet and legs warm.

Q. What food is generally given?

Gruel, simple broth, milk, etc.

Q. What will the doctor order when there is exhaustion from the fever?

Strong and stimulating nourishment.

Q. May the patient have cold water?

Cold water and weak lemonade may be given freely, unless the doctor orders differently.

Q. Where must the patient be kept?

Strictly in bed; he has to use the bed-pan and urinal.

Q. What must be guarded against especially?

Against any check of perspiration.

Q. What should be put on the patient if he is propped up in bed?

A small jacket or shawl over the night-dress, but use nothing that cannot be washed.

Q. What should be noticed at night or when the patient is sleeping?

The breathing, whether it is even and deep or short and labored, as if there was trouble with the air-passages.

Q. What must be particularly watched?

The condition of the excretions, especially the urine. Should it become scanty or smoky colored, report it at once to the doctor.

Q. What besides this should be observed?

Whether there is a free, though seemingly harmless,

discharge from the nose. This may indicate diphtheritic trouble. Or whether there is any swelling about the limbs.

Q. What must be reported to the doctor?

Every change of temperature, pulse, secretions and other symptoms.

Q. What is the peeling off process called?

Desquamation.

Q. At what time does this generally take place?

About the fifth day after the rash appears.

Q. May the patient get up during this process?

Not until this process is completed.

Q. Should the warm baths be kept up?

They should be kept up, but the least chilliness must be guarded against and the temperature of the room now allowed to be 70 degrees.

Q. How long should the patient be kept in the room?

Two weeks after the peeling is over. He should be separated not less than one month from the commencement of the disease.

Q. What care must be taken when the patient goes out the first time?

That he is well wrapped, with feet and hands protected.

Q. What maladies are likely to accompany or follow scarlet fever?

Dropsy, malignant sore throat, kidney diseases, weakness of the lungs, pleuresy and many others.

SMALLPOX.

Q. What is used as a protection against smallpox?

Vaccination.

Q. How do smallpox generally begin?

With a chill, followed by a quick pulse and high temperature of 104 to 106 degrees.

Q. Which are the distinctive symptoms?

Severe pain in the back and pit of the stomach, which increases on pressure.

Q. What do these troubles sometimes do?

They abate for awhile, but they gradually increase, and are at their height on the third day, or twelve days after exposure to the contagion.

Q. How does the eruption begin about this time?

It begins as small pimples, spreading from the face to the neck, breast and back, and then to the limbs and extremities.

Q. When does the pain pass off?

When the eruption is developed and the patient feels pretty well.

Q. When does the feeling of discomfort increase again?

As soon as suppuration begins, and the secondary fever, sometimes announced by a chill, comes on.

Q. How high does the temperature rise?

To 105 or to 106 degrees.

Q. What goes hand in hand in smallpox.

The fever and eruption.

Q. When does the patient sometimes feel relieved?

After the pimples appear, but the patient is to be treated as a very sick person through the whole course of the disease.

Q. How should the room be kept?

It should be kept dark on account of the eyes, which suffer a great deal.

Q. How should the room be ventilated?

It should be fully ventilated with an open window.

Q. How high should the temperature of the room be?

Sixty to sixty-five degrees.

Q. How should the bed covering be?

Sufficiently warm, but not heavy.

Q. What should be given for food and what for drink?

Give broths, gruel, milk, etc., as food, and cold water or lemonade for drinks.

Q. What should be done if cold compresses are ordered?

They must be rewetted by pouring fresh water over the cloths frequently.

Q. What is prescribed to prevent scars?

Keeping the face oiled, or, better than this, have strips of linen spread with simple cerate and fitted carefully over the face.

Q. How should the ordered application be used?

It must be used faithfully and the patient is to be prevented from scratching the surface, even in his sleep.

Q. What is generally necessary to accomplish this?

To tie the hands up in soft cloths, so that at least the nails may be kept from the face.

Q. What can be done if the patient is delirious or the irritation becomes unbearable?

The only thing to do is to use a shirt with very long sleeves, which you tie together at the wrist.

Dangers in the Disease.

Q. What must be carefully watched and promptly reported?

All symptoms, any light-headedness, sudden exhaustion, difficulty in swallowing, the manner of breathing, sound of the voice, etc.

Q. What complication may occur?

Pleurisy and laryngitis.

Q. When may a sister give wine—why—or brandy without waiting for orders in a smallpox case?

If during the decline of the eruption, or while the secondary fever is in progress, a clammy sweat appears or a sudden sinking of tremor.

Q. In what case should hot brandy or hot spiced drinks be given?

If the pustules sink or change to a purple color.

Disinfecting and Insolating.

Q. What should be done if the room has a carpet?

It should be taken up the first day that the disease is recognized.

Q. Should the mattresses be changed?

No, for they have already become infected.

Q. What directions should be followed about insolating the room?

The door must be locked, and no communications had with the room, except through an adjoining one where the window is down from the top and a fire, if possible, lighted.

Q. What is to be done when food, medicine, clothing, etc., are required?

The request for them should be written on a slate, which should be hung or placed where it can be read without taking it down.

Q. Where should the ordered things be brought?

To some place agreed upon, and left for the nurse to carry them into the room.

Q. What kind of bed-clothing should be used?

The oldest kind, so that they may be destroyed after the patient got well or died.

Q. What must be done with clothing that is changed?

They must be thrown into a disinfectant, which should be standing in a vessel in the adjoining room.

Q. Wherein can it best be kept?

In a wooden tub, which can be burned afterwards.

Q. How long should the clothing soak?

Twelve hours.

Q. What can be done after this?

They can be dipped out with a stick and put into hot soap suds, made with carbolic soap, and after standing two hours may be wrung out with safety and made into bundles, tossed out of a window in the yard and dried in the sun.

Q. Who can iron the clothes then?

Anybody can iron them with safety.

Q. Who should do the first soaking and rinsing?

The sister, both her own and the patient's clothing and bedding.

Q. Who should handle the articles used about the patient?

Only those who are engaged with the case.

Q. How should a sister protect herself against this disease?

By vaccination, cleanliness of clothing, by good food, sufficient rest, being relieved by an assistant, if possible.

Q. What must be done when it is necessary for her to leave the house?

A suit of fresh clothing.

Q. What should be done with the matresses after the disease?

They should be rolled up and sent to the pest house or burnt.

Q. Is this disease very contagious?

Yes; there is no disease more contagious than smallpox. It has been conveyed by infected articles carelessly put aside, opened years afterwards.

CHICKENPOX.

Q. Is chickenpox a dangerous disease?

No; it is a harmless but very annoying trouble.

Q. By what is it generally accompanied?

By a little fever and general discomfort.

Q. Where should the patient be kept?

In the house and away from other children?

Q. How should the air be in the room?

Fresh, and the temperature of the room should be kept even at 65 to 70 degrees.

Q. What kind of food should be given the first few days?

Such as broth, gruels and milk.

Q. At what time does the eruption appear?

On the first to the third day.

Q. Where is it the thickest?
On the back and chest.
Q. How should the clothing be?
Loose, so there be no irritation from rubbing.
Q. How long does the trouble generally last?
It will be over in two weeks or less.
Q. What must be done with the room afterwards?
It must be well cleaned and the mattresses sunned.

MEASLES.

Q. How does this disease begin?
It begins like a severe catarrh, with a redness and tenderness of the eyes, the light being painful to them.
Q. By what is it sometimes accompanied?
By a croupy cough.
Q. To what degree does the temperature rise?
To 101 or to 102 degrees, and the rash appears.
Q. When and where does the rash appear?
On the third or fourth day, commencing about the mouth and eyes, quickly spreading over the whole body.
Q. When does the disease generally pass off?
If the necessary precautions are observed, in two weeks.
Q. How should the room be kept?
Well ventilated and at an even temperature.
Q. With what should the temperature of the room be tested?
With a thermometer and not with the feeling.
Q. How often is the child bathed?
A warm bath is given daily and great care must be taken against getting chilled.
Q. What food is given?
Simple foods, without solids for a while; cool water to drink.
Q. How must the room be kept on account of the eyes?
It should be shaded from any bright light.

Q. Where should the patient be kept?
In bed as long as there are any indications of fever.

Q. What may exposure to draught bring on?
Pneumonia.

Q. How long should the patient be kept in the room?
As long as there is any trace left of the measles catarrh.

Q. What does this disease often bring on or leave behind it?
Pneumonia, weakness of the lungs, and bronchial catarrh.

Q. What should be brought to the doctor's attention even months after the seeming recovery?
The slightest disposition to cough or cold.

SPASMODIC CROUP.

Q. What is this disease?
It is an affection of the muscles of the windpipe, with inflammation.

Q. Who is most commonly troubled with it?
Small children. Sometimes it may trouble them when they are in the twelfth year of their age.

Q. Do relapses occur?
Very frequently.

Q. How is the patient in the intervals?
He shows little or no sign of illness.

Q. When do the spasmodic attacks mostly occur?
At night.

Q. How do they occur?
The child, being put to bed apparently well, wakes suddenly, with a croupy cough and violent choking spell, sits up in bed with an anxious face.

Q. How is the breathing?
Greatly oppressed.

Q. How long does it take before these symptoms pass off?
About two hours after treatment has commenced.

Q. How does treatment affect the patient?

The patient falls into a sleep, perspiring freely, and wakes up with but little sign of the attack.

Q. When will this trouble probably recur?

At night.

Q. How long will it be before it disappears entirely?

From three to eight days.

Q. Why must precautions be taken against simple spasmodic croup?

Because it is sometimes followed by cappilary bronchitis, which in children is an extremely dangerous disease.

Q. What must be done upon the first appearance of the attack?

The doctor must be sent for.

Q. What may be given until he comes?

Syrup of ipecac, half a teaspoonful to a child under one year, and a teaspoonful to an older child, one and one-half to a child over two years.

Q. How often can it be repeated?

In all cases it can be repeated in twenty minutes, if no vomiting occurs.

Q. What is the object of giving the ipecac?

To produce vomiting, but no violent retching.

Q. Where must a child be kept after the attack?

In a room where the thermometer stands at an even temperature of 70 degrees, not lower than 65 degrees at night.

Q. What must be avoided?

Exposure to change of temperature in passing through entries or other rooms.

Q. How must the clothing be?

Warm.

Q. What can be given for food?

Milk, gruel and broth.

Q. How long before the patient may go outdoors?

Not before all croupy sounds in breathing are over; that is from three to eight days.

Q. What weather must be avoided for croupy children?
Damp and windy weather.

MEMBRANEOUS CROUP.

Q. Is this a dangerous disease?
It is a very dangerous and usually fatal disease of the throat.

Q. By what is it characterized?
By an inflammation of the mucous membrane lining the larynx and trachea.

Q. What is found in this mucous membrane?
An effusion of fibrin.

Q. What does this fibrin do?
It coagulates on the mucous surface and forms a false membrane.

Q. What mistake is sometimes made in the commencement of this disease?
It is taken for the form of simple croup.

Q. How does the child sometimes awake?
It may suddenly wake with a croupy cough and strangling fit.

Q. What other symptoms do sometimes appear?
All symptoms of a cold in the head for a day or two, and the trouble may pass for that until the doctor is called too late.

Q. By what is the membraneous croup accompanied?
It is accompanied from the first with increasing fever.

Q. What symptoms follow the increased temperature in membraneous croup?
Loss of appetite, thirst, quick pulse, husky voice, gradually diminishing to a whisper.

Q. How is the breathing?
It comes as a sort of a whistle, with increasing effort and constant restlessness.

Q. In what does the nursing consist?
It consists in keeping up assiduously whatever reme-

dies are ordered, and sustaining the strength as long as possible.

Q. How is the atmosphere of the room to be?

Either moist or dry, as ordered by the doctor.

Q. How can you secure a moist atmosphere in a room?

It may be secured by keeping a teakettle of water boiling in the room over a spirit lamp if there is no other way.

Q. What should be done if there is a fire in the room or heat from a furnace?

Sheets should be wrung out in water and dried in the room.

Q. What is sometimes ordered to be kept in the room?

Unpainted tubs of water, and from time to time drop into them lumps of quick-lime.

Q. From what can a child easily inhale steam?

From a steam atomizer or kettle.

Q. How can it be introduced?

It can be placed so that a funnel is put over the child's face without touching it.

Q. Can a sleeping child take the vapor this way?

Yes; even better than when awake.

Q. How should the pillows be arranged?

They must be arranged so as to lift the shoulders and expand the chest.

Q. What must never press upon the child's chest?

The chin.

Q. What kind of food must be given?

Food of the most nourishing kind.

Q. What can be given for nourishment?

Beef extract, milk punch, milk with the white of an egg, one egg to every half a pint of milk shaken well.

Q. What may be given as a drink?

Cool wine-why or cold water without ice.

Q. May the child be lifted up?

Yes; it may be lifted up to ease its position.

Q. May it be taken out of bed?

Yes; it may be lifted upright in the arms or carried about in the room.

Q. What must a nurse be careful about?

She must be careful not to inhale the breath or to get particles of membrane which may be coughed up suddenly into the mouth, nose or eyes.

Q. What is the last resource taken in cases of this kind?

Tracheotomy, an operation on the windpipe, opening a passage to the lungs below the point at which the membrane is formed.

Q. What is more commonly resorted to now?

Intubation of the lungs.

Q. What is often the result of all these operations?

An unfavorable result; a large proportion of children die in spite of them.

Q. What must a sister get ready if the operation is to be performed?

A firm table, a flat pillow or a sheet folded up small to put under the head, a narrow piece of tape, scissors, needle, strong thread or silk, towels, soft sponges, tepid water, basins and a fan.

Q. What must be loosened on the patient?

Everything about the neck.

Q. What will the patient do if the operation is successfully performed and the tube introduced?

The patient, who for a moment before was choking to death, sits up, breathes freely, and all the terrible symptoms pass off for awhile.

Q. Is the danger then over?

By no means.

Q. What must therefore be kept up?

The ordered treatment, moist air, medicine and food given regularly.

Q. What must above all be taken care for?

To keep the tube perfectly clean and free from the membrane, which will be deposited in it.

Q. How can this be done?

The inner tube should be removed from the outer one every hour, or at least every two hours, and thrown into a basin of warm water?

Q. What must be done to free the tube from every particle of the membrane?

A strip of soft linen must be pushed through it with a stick.

Q. What must be done with all the membrane found in the basin?

It must be saved for the doctor's inspection.

Q. What must be watched closely?

The edges of the wound and the slightest tendency to ormation of membrane must be reported.

Q. What must be done with the creases of the skin under and about the tape which holds the tube in place?

They must be oiled to prevent chafing.

Q. What special care must be taken in regard to the mouth of the tube?

That it is not obstructed by the clothing or bedding or any particle of dust or fluff, and that no drop of water is spattered on it.

Q. How many days will determine the result?

Four or five days.

Q. Is the recovery frequent?

It is an exception, even with the greatest care.

Q. Why is recovery so seldom?

Because the membrane forms below the wound or in the lungs and suffocation follows.

Q. What must be done after recovery or death?

All precautions must be taken for disinfecting and cleaning.

DIPHTHERITIS.

Q. As what is diphtheria considered?

As a form of blood poison.

Q. From what does it often result?

From imperfect sewerage.

Q. By what is it accompanied?

By formation of membrane on the mucous surface.

Q. How does the disease begin?

It begins like so many others, with a feeling of general depression and feverishness, symptoms of cold in the head, hoarseness, difficulty in swallowing, stiffness of neck and swelling of tonsils and the glands about the throat.

Q. What will follow these symptoms if diphtheria is present?

White patches of false membrane on the tonsils and in the back of the throat.

Q. What must be done upon the first suspicion of this disease?

The patient must be insolated, kept in bed and no one allowed in the room except the attendant.

Q. How should the temperature and air be kept in the room?

The thermometer at 65-70 degrees and the room well ventilated.

Q. What may be used as a gargle?

A saturated solution of chlorate of potash.

Q. What may be given to the patient to drink?

Strong beef tea, and until this is ready, give the patient as much milk with the white of an egg as he can drink, one egg to one-half a pint.

Q. What will these precautions probably save?

They will save the patient from more severe sore throat, and in case of real diphtheria everything is done that could have been done without further instruction.

Q. What must be carried out strictly?

All orders of the doctor until the last moment, as if life depended upon the sister alone.

Q. What special precautions must be taken?

All precautions against the spread of this contagion.

Q. What will likely accompany this disease often?

An abundant, clear discharge from the mouth and nostrils.

Q. With what should it be wiped away?

With soft cloths, which are immediately burnt, as the discharges are highly infectious.

Q. With what should the lips and chin be washed?

Now and then with chlorate of potash, and keep them covered with vaseline or a little oil.

Q. For what reason must the lips and chin be treated in this manner?

Because they are touched by the discharge.

Q. What should be examined every day?

The skin must be examined everywhere and if chafed it must be treated the same as the chin and lips.

Q. What kind of food should be given?

Liquid, concentrated food, as beef tea, beef juice, egg nogg, etc.

Q. What are often ordered in this disease?

Nourishing enemas.

Q. How often should food be given?

Every hour, or oftener if the strength is failing. Follow the doctor's directions to the letter.

Q. What can be given frequently if stimulants are allowed?

Wine whey, given cold is very refreshing.

Q. What is sometimes ordered for the throat?

An atomizer or frequent swabbing of the throat.

Q. What are the greatest dangers in diphtheria?

The patient may be choked by obstruction of the throat, or paralysis of the heart may prove a fatal termination.

Q. In what position should the patient be kept?

In a horizontal position, which must be maintained for a long time.

Q. What care must be taken in convalescence?

The patient must not leave the bed or room for any purpose, or even sit up, until the doctor has given permission.

Q. What may result from carelessness in this matter?

Paralysis of the heart.

Q. What is not uncommon in convalescence from diphtheria.

Sudden death.

Q. What is affected for a long time afterwards?

The throat and power to swallow, in some cases by partial paralysis.

Q. How must a sister protect herself in cases of diphtheria?

She must be careful not to inhale the breath, and be careful about particles of mucous or membrane which may be expelled by coughing. She must have nourishing food and sufficient rest.

Q. What must be done with the sick room after the recovery or death?

The room and everything that has come in contact with the disease must be cleaned and disinfected.

Whooping Cough.

Q. How does this disease begin?

With symptoms of an ordinary cold.

Q. How soon is the peculiar whoop heard?

Not until after the tenth day.

Q. When are the paroxyisms most severe?

At night.

Q. What must be done with the child during the spasm?

It should be lifted up and as much fresh air given as possible.

Q. Is this disease dangerous?
No; it is generally harmless.
Q. What complications may arise from it?
Bronchitis or inflammation of the lungs.
Q. In what does the nursing consist?
In regulating the diet, giving unstimulating food and avoiding constipation.
Q. Should the child be allowed to go out doors?
When the weather is favorable as much time as possible should be spent out doors.
Q. How should the temperature of the room be kept?
As even as possible.
Q. How should the clothing be?
Warm in cold weather, protecting arms and chest.
Q. How long does the course of this disease run?
From six to twelve weeks.

PNEUMONIA.

Q. What is pneumonia?
It is an inflammation of the lung substance.
Q. Is it a serious disease?
It is one of the most serious pulmonary affections.
Q. In what different ways may it occur?
It may occur independently or as a complication in the course of some other disease.
Q. What does it affect?
It may affect one or both lungs, more often the right lung alone.
Q. How does the disease generally announce itself?
With a chill or chilly sensation, which may last from one-half an hour to one hour, with deep-seated pain or shortness of breath.
Q. What follows the chill?
A high temperature of 103 to 105 degrees, with flushed face, often on one side only, headache and restlessness.

Q. Which is the first decided symptom of pneumonia?
Shortness of breath.

Q. What must be especially noticed?
The expectoration; a sputa cup should always be used and the sputa be saved for the doctor's inspection.

Q. How is the expectoration generally in the beginning?
Scanty and clear.

Q. When may it be expected to increase in quantity?
After twelve to eighteen hours.

Q. What character does it assume by this time?
It becomes tough and tenacious.

Q. What color does it sometimes show?
A rusty color or streaks of blood.

Q. How is the cough?
Short and hacking.

Q. What must be observed besides this?
The breathing during the sleep, whether the patient feels pain when lying in one position more than in another.

Q. How is the breathing generally?
Shallow and rapid.

Q. What more should be noticed?
The character and quantity of urine.

Q. How is the urine generally?
Scanty and high-colored.

Q. When does the disease reach its height?
At the end of the first week.

Q. What will occur at the end of the first week in ordinary cases?
The critical day, or crisis.

Q. Are patients with pneumonia often delirious?
Yes, especially at night.

Q. What is always the great danger in this disease?
Heart failure.

Q. How must the patient be kept for this reason?
Absolutely quiet and in bed.

Q. How should the patient's strength be kept up?

By not allowing unnecessary talking or exertion, and by giving nourishment and stimulants frequently.

Q. What kind of food is generally given?

Liquid but nourishing food.

Q. How often should the patient be fed?

At least every two hours, and a little at the time.

Q. What applications are sometimes ordered in pneumonia?

A counter-irritant, cotton jacket, priessnits poultice, linseed poultice or jacket, leeches or canthos plaster.

Q. How should the temperature of the room be kept?

The same during day and night—65 or 70 degrees—and as even as possible.

Q. What kind of water is used for bathing?

Tepid, unless ordered different by the doctor.

Q. What special precautions must be taken?

1. To guard the patient in every way against draught.
2. Keep feet and legs warm.
3. Never expose the patient by throwing back the covers, not even for a moment.

Q. How should the patient be supported to ease his breathing?

By pillows under his shoulders.

Q. What must be put around the patient during this upright position?

A wrap around the shoulders.

PHTHISIS OR PULMONARY CONSUMPTION.

Q. Is this disease fatal?

It is almost always fatal sooner or later.

Q. By what is it characterized?

By a morbid deposit of tubercles in the lungs.

Q. Will these tubercles nodules only attack the lungs?

No; they may also attack other parts of the body and have a great tendency to spread.

Q. Is this disease infectious?

Without doubt.

Q. What will favor its development?

Exposure, overwork and intemperance.

Q. How do the attacks come on?

Either acute, terminating in a few weeks, or chronic, lasting for several years.

Q. At what age does it most commonly attack persons?

Persons under thirty years of age.

Q. Which are its most characteristic symptoms?

Cough, fever, night sweats, spitting of blood, gastric derangements, loss of appetite, gradually losing flesh and increasing weakness.

Q. What does sometimes occur during the disease?

Periods of apparent improvement, but they are rarely permanent.

Q. From what does the patient finally die?

From hemorrhage or exhaustion.

Q. What may sometimes relieve the distressing symptoms.

Good treatment.

Q. Is there no remedy or treatment to arrest for sure the progress of the disease?

It has not been discovered yet.

Q. What will sometimes exert a beneficial influence on the patient?

Change of climate.

Q. Where should the patient spend a great deal of his time in case the weather is pleasant?

In the open air.

Q. What kind of atmosphere is the most desirable for him?

A dry atmosphere, with plenty of sun and free from wind.

Q. What must be avoided above all things?

Over-crowding and defective ventilation.

Q. What diet should be given?
Liberal and nourishing diet.
Q. What should be used for the sputa?
Always a cup, in which a solution of bichloride should be kept constantly and besides this the cups should be frequently boiled.
Q. For what reason?
Because the germs of the disease are largely contained in the expectoration, and if allowed to dry and evaporate will be inhaled by others.
Q. What precautions should be taken?
That dishes, etc., that are used by consumptives should be kept separate for them alone.
Q. What care must be taken about clothes?
That everything is thoroughly cleaned and disinfected before it is used by anyone else.

PLEURISY.

Q. What is pleurisy?
It is an inflammation of the serous membrane covering the lungs.
Q. How do the surfaces of the membrane become?
Dry and no longer slide easily over each other.
Q. What is felt upon inspiration?
Acute pain.
Q. How is the cough?
Short and repressed.
Q. What other symptoms occur?
Inability to draw a long breath and some elevation of temperature.
Q. By what are these symptoms sometimes preceded?
By a sense of chilliness?
Q. By what may the pain be relieved?
By external applications of counter-irritants.
Q. What is sometimes applied for support?
Strips of adhesive plaster over one side or both sides of the chest, and back.

Q. What may take place if the inflammation continues?
An effusion of fluid in the pleural cavity.

Q. If this fluid becomes abundant upon what does it act embarrassing?
Upon the action of the heart and lungs.

Q. What is generally necessary to relieve this condition?
Aspiration of the fluid.

Q. What do you understand by aspirating?
An operation which consists in drawing off the fluid through a hollow needle made for that purpose and attached to an aspirator.

Q. What must always be done with this fluid?
It must be saved for examination.

Q. What will be found in some cases in the place of fluid?
An accumulation of pus.

Q. What is this form of pleurisy called?
Epyema.

Q. What will be necessary in this case?
A free opening and a thorough draining of the pleural cavity.

Q. What may be necessary in some cases?
That the cavity and tube be washed with an antiseptic solution and the dressings changed as needed.

Cholera Morbus.

Q. By what is this disease caused?
By the use of indigestible food, stale meats or fish, impure drinking water, etc.

Q. What symptoms occur?
Vomiting and purging of liquid matter and bile in quantities.

Q. Where has the patient violent pain?
In the stomach, cramps in the legs and muscles of the abdomen, coldness and faintness.

Q. To what has the patient a tendency?
To collapse.

Q. How does the attack come on?
Suddenly.

Q. What should not be done at first?
The vomiting and purging should not be checked.

Q. Why?
Because this would prevent nature from getting rid of an irritant.

Q. What should be given if the skin becomes cold and the pulse feeble?
A tablespoon of brandy in a wine glass of hot water.

Q. What may be applied to relieve pain in the stomach?
Mustard plaster, which should be mixed with hot water.

Q. What other applications may be used?
Wring out a flannel in hot water, sprinkle turpentine over it and apply.

Q. What is this application called?
A turpentine stupe.

Q. What may be the consequence if these applications are left on too long?
They may blister and must therefore be watched.

Q. What should be done if there are cramps in the legs?
They must be rubbed vigorously.

Q. Where must the patient be kept?
In bed with hot bottles to the feet if they are cold.

Q. Is cholera morbus fatal?
It is seldom fatal, but it is prostrating.

Q. What kind of food should the patient take after the attack?
Light, but nourishing food.

Q. Of what may this consist?
Milk and rice gruel, strong broth, beef tea and eggs, if allowed by the doctor.

Q. How should the return to solid food be?
Gradually.

Q. What will probably be ordered if the bowels do not move readily?

An enema of warm water and oil of glycerine.

ASIATIC CHOLERA.

Q. By what is this disease generally communicable?

By the excretions.

Q. By what is this disease characterized?

By violent vomiting and purging of rice, watery evacuations, cramps, extreme prostrations and collapse.

Q. How does it usually commence?

With slight diarrhoea and nausea.

Q. What symptoms appear soon if it is really Asiatic cholera?

Intense thirst, restlessness and muscular spasms.

Q. How does the pulse become?

Rapid and weak.

Q. How is the temperature?

It falls below normal.

Q. The skin?

It becomes livid.

Q. The eye-balls?

Sunken.

Q. What generally precedes death?

A ghastly appearance.

Q. How long is the mind clear?

Usually to the end.

Q. What is generally given first to control the purging?

Opium.

Q. Where must the patient be kept?

Insolated, in bed and warm.

Q. In what position should the patient be kept in cholera?

In a recumbent position, that is flat on the back.

Q. What may be given for the intense thirst?

Ice at liberty, but little water.

Q. What food?
Strictly what has been ordered by the doctor.
Q. What may become necessary to keep up the strength?
Nourishing enemas.
Q. What must be done with stools, vomited matter and urine?
They must be disinfected thoroughly and disposed of promptly.
Q. What precautions must be taken?
All possible precautions against spreading the disease.

DIARRHŒA.

Q. What does the word signify?
To flow through.
Q. By what is this disease characterized?
By profuse discharge from the bowels.
Q. How may the trouble be brought on?
In various ways.
Q. Which are the commonest ways?
Imprudence in eating and drinking.
Q. What may produce the disease?
Unripe fruit, badly cooked vegetables, impurities in drinking water, over-fatigue, and sometimes grief or fright.
Q. What will generally effect a cure?
Rest in bed and fasting entirely for one day.
Q. What will this rest and fasting give to the stomach and intestines?
It will give the stomach time to get rid of the irritating substances and the intestines a rest, by having no work to do.
Q. What may be given if the patient begins to feel hungry?
Boiled rice and milk, corn-starch gruel or arrow root, and return slowly to solid food.
Q. What should be done if the trouble continues in spite of this treatment?
The physician should be consulted.

DYSENTERY.

Q. What is this disease?

An inflammation of the mucous membrame of the larger intestines.

Q. What are the symptoms?

Griping pain in the abdomen, bloody discharges from the bowels, constant desire to use the night-chair and straining.

Q. How should the vessels be kept?

Disinfected.

Q. What must be done with evacuations?

They must at once be carried out of the room.

Q. How should the air be kept?

Fresh, by free ventilation.

Q. What should be kept in the room?

Some disinfectant, as chloride of lime mixed with water.

Q. How much fluid shall be given if enemas are ordered?

Not more than four or five ounces at a time.

Q. What should be put around the abdomen?

A wide flannel bandage.

Q. How shall the patient be kept?

Flat on his back and perfectly quiet, until all traces of the disease are gone.

Q. What food is given?

Boiled beef and cooled, never too hot.

INTESTINAL COLIC.

Q. By what is this most commonly caused?

By constipation and flatulence.

Q. Of what character is the pain?

It is severe and griping.

Q. In what way is this pain distinguished from that of peritonitis?

That it is relieved by pressure, while the latter is increased by pressure.

Q. What will generally afford entire relief?
A clearing out of the bowels.
Q. How is this most safely accomplished?
By enema.
Q. What may be helpful in relieving the pain?
A hot drink, hot applications externally and massage of the abdomen.

HEPATIC COLIC.

Q. To what is this trouble generally due?
To the presence of a gallstone in the biliary duct.
Q. Where does an agonizing pain come to?
To the upper part of the right abdomen.
Q. What does this pain produce?
Faintness, nausea and profuse perspiration.
Q. In what case will the attack subside?
Only in that case, that the obstructing stone passes on into the intestine.
Q. What may be used to relieve the pain?
Hypodermic injections of morphia and hot fomentations sprinkled with laudanum.
Q. From what does this attack result?
From a diseased condition of the liver.
Q. By what are the attacks often followed?
By jaundice.
Q. By what is jaundice marked?
By a yellow tinge of the skin and the whites of the eyes.
Q. What often accompanies jaundice?
Great depression of spirit, loss of appetite, nausea and extreme itching of the skin.

GASTRITIS.

Q. What is gastritis?
It is an inflammation of the mucuous membrane of the stomach.

Q. Where does this cause burning pain?
In the pit of the stomach.

Q. What other symptoms accompany them?
Vomiting on eating or drinking, and sometimes hiccough.

Q. How does it affect the patient?
The patient is pale and faint, with cold extremities and damp skin.

Q. How does the patient's skin become?
Weak and feeble.

Q. What does especially cause him pain?
The movements of the diaphragm, and consequently the breathing is short.

Q. From what will the patient suffer at times?
From tormenting thirst, although the water drank is vomited at once.

Q: By what may the disease be brought on?
By taking any substance into the stomach which in itself is poisonous, or becomes so.

Q. How should the patient be kept?
At rest, absolutely in bed.

Q. What may be given as a drink?
Cold water, if it can be retained.

Q. What must be done if enemas are ordered?
They must be given gently and disturb the patient's position as little as possible.

Q. What are the general rules for administering food?
To give the food in small quantities frequently.

Q. To what should the diet be confined?
To milk diluted with lime water, two tablespoonsful to a half pint of milk.

Q. How should this be commenced?
Give a teaspoonful once in half an hour.

Q. When may this be increased to a dessertspoonful?
If the milk is retained for two or three hours.

Q. What should be gradually increased?

The dose: lengthen the intervals, until two tablespoonsful can be taken every two hours.

Q. In what case must the dose be omitted?

On the slightest feeling of nausea or belching of wind.

Q. What is always more advisable in regard to food?

To shorten the intervals between the doses than to increase the dose suddenly.

Q. To what food may you gradually go from milk?

To thin gruel, made very smooth, of rice flour, arrow root or corn starch.

Indigestion or Dyspepsia.

Q. What is indigestion or dyspepsia?

It may be merely a slight functional disorder or a symptom of a serious disease.

Q. By what symptoms may it be accompanied?

By pain, nausea, regurgitation, flatulence, palpitation, headache, constipation or diarrhœa.

Q. What are dyspeptics noted for?

For constantly studying their symptoms.

Q. What is a common cause of indigestion?

Food in unsuitable quality or quantity.

Q. What does often produce it?

Over fatigue may often produce it, but alcoholism always does produce it?

Q. Why can no general rules be laid down for treatment in this disease?

Because what suits one case will not suit another.

Q. What is, therefore, first necessary?

To discover the cause of the trouble and treat accordingly.

Q. What is always important for dyspeptics?

Exercise in the fresh air and simple food.

PERITONITIS.

Q. What is peritonitis?

It is an inflammation of the membrane which lines the abdominal cavity.

Q. By what is it generally caused?

By wounds or diseases of the abdomen, or organs covered by the peritoneum.

Q: What are the symptoms?

Acute pain, with tenderness over the abdomen, fever, rapid wiry pulse, great depression, vomiting and constipation with tympanites.

Q. What effects has the disease upon the urine?

Retention or suppression of urine.

Q. What is not uncommon?

Delirium.

Q. How should the patient be kept?

As quiet as possible and not allowed to sit up for any purpose.

Q. By what should the bed clothes be supported?

By a cradle.

Q. What special care must be taken if applications or fomentations are ordered?

To make them as light as possible.

Q. What nourishment may be given?

Strictly according to orders of the doctor, usually liquids.

Q. What must be kept warm?

The knees and feet.

Q. What must be watched in case opium is ordered?

The respirations.

Q. What should be daily looked after?

That the bowels are kept open.

Q. What should be worn next to the abdomen?

A flannel bandage.

Q. What will be a sure consequence of too early an exertion?

A relapse.

APPENDICITIS.

Q. What is appendicitis?

It is an inflammation of the vermiform appendix.

Q. By what is it usual y accompanied?

By more or less peritonitis.

Q. What are the symptoms and what is the treatment?

Much the same as peritonitis.

Q. What great danger is always to be feared in this disease?

Perforation of the bowels.

Q. How is appendicitis often treated?

By an operation of the laporatomy.

SORE THROAT.

Q. What does a slight sore throat often accompany?

Indigestion, constipation and colds.

Q. How can a slight sore throat be treated?

Regulate the bowels, eat light food for a day or so, gargle the throat with a saturated solution of chloride of potash.

Q. Where should the patient be kept and what should he avoid?

He should be kept in the house, but avoid hot, unventilated rooms.

Q. What should be used about the throat?

Cold water should be used freely about the throat, wring out a towel in strong salt water and rub the throat and chest well.

BRONCHITIS.

Q. What is bronchitis?

It is an inflammation of the bronchial tubes.

Q. In what form may it appear?

Either acute or chronic.

Q. How does the acute bronchitis begin?

It begins with a heavy cold. sometimes with a slight chill.

Q. What other symptoms appear?
There is a fullness in the head, sore throat and general sick feeling, with pain in the chest and cough.

Q. How is the cough?
At first it is dry, then it is accompanied by watery sputa, later on it becomes tough (viscid) and like purulent.

Q. What may arise in case the dysponea (difficulty in breathing) increases?
High fever, rapid pulse and profuse perspiration.

Q. Where must the patient be kept?
In one room, well aired, and at an even temperature not higher than 68 degrees.

Q. What must be secured?
A free action of the skin and the bowels open.

Q. What may relieve the pain in the chest?
A mustard plaster.

Q. What will allay the cough?
Steam inhalation.

Q. What nourishment should be given?
Plenty of light but nourishing food.

Q. What special care must be taken during convalescence?
To avoid sudden changes of temperature.

Q. For what reason?
Because the patient is very susceptible to chills.

Q. What may be looked for in the majority of cases?
Recovery.

Q. How does it prove sometimes?
Fatal or it may assume a chronic form.

ASTHMA.

Q. What is asthma?
It is a difficulty in breathing (dysponea).

Q. By what is it caused?
By a spasmodic contraction of the bronchial tubes.

Q. What is necessary for a sister to know about this disease?
The popular remedies in case of emergency.

Q. Is this disease dangerous?

It is seldom dangerous but always distressing.

Q. What are the symptoms at the time of the attack?

The patient gasps violently for air, his expression is anxious, pulse feeble, the skin cold and pale or blue.

Q. What should be done with the patient?

His arms should be elevated and all possible fresh air given him.

Q. What may be administered to the patient?

A teaspoonful of Hoffman's anodyne and repeated after half an hour if the condition is not relieved.

Q. How long may it last?

Several hours.

Q. By what is it generally concluded?

By a paroxysm of coughing and a free expectoration of mucous.

Q. What else besides this will often give relief?

Saltpeter pestelles, when burned, afford fumes, which may give relief by inhaling the fumes.

Q. What is sometimes used for smoking, either in cigarettes or pipe?

Stamonium.

LARYNGITIS.

Q. What is laryngitis?

It is an inflammation of the lining membrane of the throat, extending into the larynx.

Q. What may cause it?

Cold or local irritation.

Q. What is often associated with it?

Tuberculous disease.

Q. Which are the symptoms?

Hoarseness of voice, sore throat, usually some fever and sometimes difficulty in breathing.

Q. How is it generally treated?

By steam-inhalions.

CATARRH.

Q. What is catarrh?
It is a cold in the head.

Q. What is much responsible for the susceptibility to colds?
Illy-ventilated rooms and over-heated houses.

Q. Which are the best preventives?
Pure air, warm clothing and dry feet.

Q. What will sometimes cure the cold?
A full dose of quinine, if taken in the earliest stage.

Q. What will often cut it short?
Ten grains of dovers powder, taken at bed time.

Q. How long does it usually last?
A few days.

Q. By what may the discharge from the nose be relieved?
By inhaling through a paper cone the vapors arising from a solution of pulverized camphor or compound tincture of bezoin.

Q. What is very difficult to overcome?
Neglected cold after it has gone into a condition of chronic catarrh.

Q. What may it finally lead to?
To dangerous pulmonary diseases.

Q. What is a peculiar mark of chronic catarrh?
Strong and offensive odor.

DROPSY.

Q. What are some of the symptoms of dropsy?
An accumulation of fluid under the skin and in the cavities of the body and shortness of breath.

Q. Where does a large amount of this fluid sometimes accumulate?
In the peritoneal cavity.

Q. What will this produce?
Great distention of the abdomen.

Q. With what will it interfere?
With movements of the diaphragm.

Q. By what must the fluid be removed?
By tapping.

Q. What does fluid in the connective tissues produce?
It produces a swelling (oedema).

Q. Where will this be most marked?
Where the skin is lose.

Q. What will pressure of the finger make upon this swelling?
A distinct indention, which does not immediately disappear when pressure is removed.

Q. How is this swelling reduced sometimes?
By tapping the skin with a needle.

Q. What is necessary after this tapping?
That the discharging fluid be absorbed in soft cloths.

Q. What position can such patients most easily acquire?
Sitting up as straight as possible.

Q. How should the feet be kept while sitting up?
Elevated.

Q. What food is generally given?
Mostly liquids, no eggs; milk freely.

BRIGHT'S DISEASE.

Q. What is Bright's disease?
Several varieties of kidney trouble.

Q. What is present in the urine?
Albumen.

Q. From what does the condition commonly described as acute Bright's disease result?
From taking cold, or as a sequel of scarlet fever, diphtheria or rheumatism.

Q. How is the urine passed?
It is passed frequently, but diminishes in quantity.

Q. How is the complexion?
Waxy.

Q. About what part of the body can a dropsical condition be noticed at first?
About the eyes and feet.

Q. What other symptoms may be looked for?
Headache, gastric disorders and general debility.
Q. What are frequent complications?
Bronchitis and heart disease.
Q. What may follow?
Suppression of urine, leading to death by uræmic convulsions.
Q. How may the disease terminate?
To recovery or lapse into a chronic form.
Q. What is done to carry off the waste product from the kidneys?
The skin action is excited, the bowels are kept open and drinks given freely.
Q. What are sometimes prescribed?
Hot air baths and also skimmed milk diet.
Q. What food can be allowed?
Only digestible food and given with the utmost regularity.
Q. What must be especially avoided?
All stimulants, eggs: meat, very little, no pork.

Renal Colic.

Q. Where does the pain take its origin in renal colic?
In the kidney.
Q. Of what is it generally the result?
Of a stone in the kidney or ureter.
Q. How is the urine?
It may be retained or discharged frequently, a few drops at a time.
Q. What does the urine often contain?
Blood or crystalline deposit.
Q. By what can the pain be relieved?
Only by hypodermic of morphine.
Q. What may sometimes be ordered?
Hot baths or hot applications.

Nettle Rash or Urticaris.

Q. How does this rash appear?

It shows patches of white spots on a red ground on various parts of the body, with severe itching.

Q. By what is it produced?

By irritation, indigestible food, by certain drugs and even occasionally by strong emotions.

Q. With what may it be treated?

With applications of tincture of benzoine diluted.

Eczema.

Q. What is eczema?

It is a form of eruption very difficult to cure.

Q. Is there only one form of eczema?

No; there are various forms of it, acute or chronic.

Q. Which is the most characteristic manifestation?

A raw surface, with moist perspiration, from broken blisters, more or less covered with dry crusts.

Q. What must be done before any curative treatment will be of service?

The crusts must be softened with oil (vaseline) and gently removed.

Q. With what may the affected parts be cleaned?

With soft potash soap, and then healing ointment applied.

Q. What should be avoided?

Washing with ordinary soap and water, as well as scratching or any rubbing.

Herpes.

Q. What is this disease?

It is an eruption of small blisters, of which there are several forms.

Q. Which is the form most generally known?

Herpes zoster or shingles.

Q. Where does it appear?

On the chest.

Q. To where does it extend?

Just half way round from the spinal column to the sternum.

Q. To where is it almost always confined?

To one side.

Q. By what is the eruption preceded?

By pain of a neuralgic character.

Q. How long may the pain continue?

Even some time after the blisters have appeared.

Q. What may be done to relieve it?

Soothing application applied.

Q. How long will it take before the disease will terminate?

It is self-limited and will terminate in a few days without treatment.

ITCH OR SCABIES.

Q. To what is this disease due?

To a small animal, which burrows under the skin.

Q. What does it set up?

A peculiar irritating inflammation.

Q. Where does it usually begin?

Between the fingers and toes, but may spread to other parts of the body and become quite general.

Q. With what is it commonly treated?

With sulphur baths and sulphur ointment.

Q. Is it contagious?

It is highly contagious and persons affected with it should be insolated until cured.

Q. What should be done with their clothes afterwards?

They should be disinfected by fumigating with sulphur.

CEREBRAL APOPLEXY.

Q. By what is it caused?

By rupture of blood vessels, or an effusion of blood into the tissues of the brain.

Q. In what age is it more common?

It is more common before forty years than after.

Q. How may the attack come on?

Suddenly, the patient falling to the ground without warning, and lying without sense or motion.

Q. How is the face, pulse and breathing?

The face is flushed, the pulse free, the breathing noisy as in a deep sleep.

Q. What may follow?

Death may follow at once or the patient revives from the attack.

Q. What may sometimes precede the attack?

Warnings, such as a sudden sharp pain in the head, with confusion and dizziness.

Q. How may the second form of the attack come on?

The patient slides to the ground, fainting and pale.

Q. What does the patient generally do?

He revives from this condition.

Q. But what will generally happen after a few minutes?

The patient falls into a stupor from which he never awakes.

Q. Which of the two attacks is the most serious?

The second.

Q. What should be done with the patient if an attack in the first form occurs, until the doctor comes?

He should be put in a half-sitting position, shoulders and head raised, cold cloths applied to the head, and everything tight about the throat and body loosened.

Q. How should the room be kept?

Cool and quiet.

Q. What is to be done in the second form?

The head and shoulders of the patient are raised as in the first, but the patient's skin being cold, hot bottles should be applied to the legs and feet, and free ventilation given.

Q. What should be given if it is possible to make the patient swallow?

Fifteen to twenty drops of aromatic spirits of ammonia in a half-glass of water, given slowly.

Q. What food is given to the patient if he recovers from the attack?

Unstimulating, but nourishing: no malt or spirits are allowed.

Q. How must exercise be taken?

Without heating the body.

Q. Against what must be guarded?

Against all exertion which flushes the face.

Q. Is a bath allowed?

No hot or cold plunge bath is allowed.

Q. What may be used instead?

A tepid sponging daily is best, but the head should not be held down over the basin.

Q. What must be especially avoided?

All bodily and mental excitement.

PARALYSIS.

Q. By what may it be caused?

By apoplexy.

Q. How does it occur?

In several forms; either one side of the body is attacked or the lower half.

Q. How does it come on?

Either suddenly or by a gradual loss of motion or sensation, or of both in one or more parts of the body.

Q. What is often the end of paralysis?

Sudden death.

Q. What symptoms do sometimes occur?

Remarkable rise of temperature.

Q. To what is there a very marked tendency in this disease?

To the formation of bed sores.

Q. What danger often remains even if the patient survives?

That the attacks recur and the patient rarely revives from more than two or three attacks.

Q. What is often the main cause of paralysis?

Chronic alcoholism, poisoning or a sequel of some other disease.

Q. What kind of diet is given to the patient?

Liberal diet.

Q. What is usually employed?

Massage and electricity.

Q. How must the paralyzed parts be kept?

Warm, clean and free from pressure.

Q. What is often of the utmost importance in all these cases?

Good nursing, much skill and great patience.

Neuralgia.

Q. What is neuralgia?

It is an acute, painful affection of the nerves without inflammation.

Q. What causes it?

The causes are various and the treatment therefore different.

Q. What may be useful?

Hot applications.

Epilepsy.

Q. Among what diseases is this classed?

Among nervous diseases.

Q. How does the attack come on?

The patient apparently well the moment before, suddenly falls to the ground, frothing at the mouth, and sometimes uttering a strange cry.

Q. How is the breathing?

Difficult and the body convulsed.

Q. How is the face?
Contorted and livid, and there is a choking sound in the throat?
Q. How long will these frightful symptoms last?
They will pass off in awhile and the patient lies stupid.
Q. How long does it take before he recovers?
A few hours.
Q. How does the attack come on in a milder form?
The patient loses consciousness for a moment, does not fall, has fixed look of the eye.
Q. How long is it before he revives?
Almost immediately.
Q. How may it affect the patient?
The patient may turn pale and slide down quietly without making any sound; is insensible.
Q. How will the patient be after he revives?
He is confused and languid for the rest of the day.
Q. Do these attacks return frequently?
Sometimes at shorter or longer intervals; sometimes several times a day.
Q. Where should the patient be put if the attack comes?
In the middle of the bed.
Q. What should be done in case he cannot be moved?
He should be left lying on the floor, his head raised, his clothing unfastened.
Q. What can be done to prevent the tongue from being bitten?
Something should be placed between the teeth.
Q. What may be applied to the forehead?
Cloths dipped in cold water.
Q. How should the feet be kept?
Warm.
Q. How should the room be kept?
Darkened and quiet.
Q. How should people live that are liable to this disease?
Their manner of living should be quiet and very plain.

Q. What should they avoid chiefly?

All heating exercise, or going up and down stairs, or doing anything that creates dizziness.

Q. Where should they spend as much time as possible?

In the open air, and as little as possible over books and in business.

Q. What should they eat?

Easily digested and nourishing food, and that slowly.

HYSTERIA.

Q. What is hysteria?

It is the name given to a disordered state of the nervous system.

Q. In whom is it most common?

In girls and young women, though not entirely confined to them.

Q. What do these patients generally do?

They exaggerate more or less intentionally their symptoms.

Q. But what should be remembered?

That at the basis of these imaginative manifestations is a real, though perhaps obscure malady.

Q. To what may hysteria lead?

To insanity.

Q. What are the common symptoms?

A sensation as a ball in the throat, a dry cough, very abundant and light colored urine, flatulence.

Q. What does sometimes occur?

Neuralgia, local paralysis, contraction of the joints and loss of voice.

Q. In what way does a hysterical fit differ from an attack of epilepsy?

Hysterical patients scream repeatedly when the fit comes on, which epileptics do not.

Q. What will they never allow to be touched?

Their eye-lids.

Q. To what are they very sensitive?
To the touch.
Q. Are they stupid and dull after the fit?
They are rather drowsy.
Q. What should be done with hysterical patients?
They should be put on the bed, the clothes loosened.
Q. With what may the chest and face be slapped?
With the ends of a towel which has been dipped in cold water.
Q. What will the patient never do if left alone?
Hurt herself.
Q. How are such patients sometimes successfully treated?
By rest, seclusion, dieting, massage, electricity and sponging.
Q. What does a nurse need for these things?
Special training and experience.
Q. Can any sister undertake to practice massage?
Not without having received a thorough training and instruction in it.
Q. Can any sister practice electrical treatments?
Never unless she is well informed about it and distinctly directed by the doctor.
Q. Why?
Because electricity is a powerful agent that can do much harm, and therefore requires the greatest care and management.

Chorea or St. Vitus Dance.

Q. What is St. Vitus dance?
It is a nervous affection.
Q. In whom does it most frequently occur?
In young girls.
Q. By what is it brought on sometimes?
By fright or excitement.
Q. With what is it often associated?
With rheumatism.

Q. By what is it characterized?
By lack of control of the muscular movements.
Q. Where does it affect the body?
On one or both sides.
Q. By what is this generally accompanied?
By general debility, and often mental weakness.
Q. By what are the jerking and twitching motions increased?
By any excitement.
Q. When do these motions cease?
During sleep.
Q. What are common complications of this disease?
Bed sores.
Q. What is essential in treatment?
Complete bodily and mental rest and nourishing food.

CEREBRAL MENINGITIS.

Q. What is this disease?
It is an inflammation of the membrane covering the brain and is always extremely serious.
Q. Which are the leading symptoms?
High fever, violent headache, intolerance of light and noise, vomiting, obstinate constipation, delirium, sometimes loss of speech and convulsions.
Q. What is generally first ordered?
Cold applications to the head.
Q. How can they be most easily applied?
By means of an ice bag.
Q. What should be done to increase the effect of this application?
The head should be shaved.
Q. What else is frequently ordered?
Leeches.
Q. What is generally ordered to relieve the obstinate constipation?
Purgatives and high-up enemas.

Q. How should the patient be kept?

In a darkened room, as quiet, cool and free from excitement as possible.

Q. What kind of food should be given?

Only such as is permitted by the doctor, which is generally milk or thin gruel.

Q. How long must the patient and room be kept quiet?

Until all possibility of a relapse is over.

Q. What does relapse in this case mean?

Death.

Q. In what cases may a sister on her own account give an ounce of wine in hot water or beef tea?

If there should be symptoms of sinking, cold sweat, fixed and glassy eyes, stupor, palsy.

Q. What other symptoms do appear in spinal meningitis?

Excessive pain in the back, extending to the extremities.

Q. How does the body become?

It becomes rigid, but from time to time there are convulsive starts.

Q. How are the lower limbs affected?

By paralysis, which gradually extends.

Q. What can be done in such a case?

Nothing but to follow the directions of the doctor?

Q. What treatment is sometimes performed by the doctor?

A lumbar puncture.

Q. What else is often ordered?

Leeches, cups and bichloride injections.

Q. How is a bichloride injection given?

Have a special syringe for it, mix the bichloride with the water in a glass or porcelain dish, then add salt as much as the water (in which the bichloride is dissolved) will dissolve. Then have everything ready and put the bichloride into the syringe at the side of the bed and inject at once deep under the muscles. The syringe must be cleaned at once.

RHEUMATISM.

Q. From what does inflammatory rheumatism or acute rheumatic fever result?

From exposure to cold and damp.

Q. By what is it characterized?

By inflammation of the white fibrous about the joints and in the wall of the large arteries and valves of the heart.

Q. By what may it possibly be developed?

By malarial poisoning.

Q. Which are the local symptoms in the acute form?

Fever-heat, redness, swelling and pain about one or more of the large joints.

Q. To what has this a tendency?

To shift from joint to joint.

Q. By what are these symptoms accompanied?

By profuse perspiration, having a characteristic odor.

Q. How is the urine?

It is likely to be scanty and high-colored.

Q. What may accompany severe cases?

Nervous disorders and mild delirium at night.

Q. In what does the greatest danger consist?

That the heart gets involved.

Q. What position should be maintained?

A horizontal position.

Q. Why?

Because the slightest emotion causes an agonizing pain.

Q. What must be avoided?

All excitement, and in no case stimulants are given except when ordered by the doctor.

Q. What kind of food may be given?

Light, digestible food.

Q. How should the patient be dressed?

Warmly in flannel.

Q. When the case has become chronic, where should the patient then live if possible?

In a dry climate.

Q. What must be carefully avoided?
Sudden change of temperature.

Q. On what days must the patient not go out?
On cold, damp days.

Q. What kind of underwear should the patient wear?
Flannel from throat to ankles, summer and winter.

POINTS TO BE NOTICED IN GIVING STIMULANTS IN FEVERS.

Q. When may stimulants be recognized as helpful to the patient?
If after taking them, the tongue and skin becomes moist, the pulse steadier, the breathing more tranquil, delirium quieted, sleep induced.

Q. When are they doing harm?
If the reverse effects follow, the tongue and skin becoming dry, the pulse quicker, the breathing hurried.

Q. What must be done in this case?
They must be stopped.

MALARIAL OR INTERMITTENT FEVER.

Q. What does the most common form of this fever exhibit?
Three stages.

Q. With what is the patient first seized?
With a chill, more or less violent and prolonged.

Q. How does he feel during this time?
Cold, but the temperature rises rapidly.

Q. What other symptoms appear?
Severe headache, nausea and pain in the limbs.

Q. By what is the feeling of chilliness succeeded?
By a hot stage.

Q. What symptoms accompany this stage?
High temperature, flushed face, dry and hot skin.

Q. What will finally, perhaps after a few hours, follow?
Profuse sweating, during which the temperature falls and the other acute symptoms subside.

Q. How do the attacks occur?
Periodically, with intervals of fairly good feeling.
Q. What is required for this disease?
Constitutional treatment and sometimes change of climate?
Q. What can a nurse do during the chill?
She can relieve the discomfort by the use of warm blankets, hot bottles, etc.
Q. How can she relieve the fever?
By tepid sponging and cooling drinks.

TEMPERATURE, PULSE, RESPIRATIONS AND URINE.

Q. What vital signs are more or less intimately connected in sickness?
Temperature, pulse and respirations.
Q. What is the cause of this connection?
That what affects one will also affect the other.
Q. Which of the three are the more readily disturbed?
The pulse and respirations.
Q. Which of these symptoms expresses more correctly the condition of the patient?
The variations of the temperature.
Q. What causes often alterations in the pulse and respirations with children?
Sleep, anger, suckling and slight indigestion.
Q. Are these respirations of great importance?
Not unless accompanied with changes in the temperature.
Q. In whom are the variations more important?
In adults.
Q. Which is the normal temperature of adults?
Ninety-eight and four to six-tenths degrees.
Q. What should, therefore, be carefully noted in adults?
The first variation from the normal temperature.
Q. Is this deviation in all cases of special importance?
No: if it is only for a day.

Q. What is a sure sign that there is probably something wrong?

If the temperature on the morning of the second day is higher than the first, and by noon still higher.

Q. For what does an increase of temperature call?

For cooling remedies, external and internal.

Q. What does a decrease of temperature require?

Warming and sustaining treatment.

Q. What must be carefully noticed?

The hour at which the rise or fall of temperature takes place.

Q. What is a bad sign in the increase of temperature?

If the increase begins a little earlier each day.

Q. What is a more favorable sign?

If it begins a little later every day.

Q. What is a good sign in the decrease in temperature?

If the decrease begins a little later every day.

Q. What is a bad indication?

If it begins later each day.

Q. What else is important to consider in regard to temperature?

The duration.

Q. What is a bad sign in the duration?

A long continued high temperature without a fall.

Q. What is an encouraging sign?

A long continued low temperature.

Q. What is dangerous in itself regarding temperature?

A very high temperature, say 105 degrees.

Q. In what case is it more dangerous?

If it has come on gradually as the last of a progressive series, the temperature having grown daily higher by half a degree or more, and having become daily higher by an hour or so earlier.

Q. What should a fall from a high temperature below the normal point, say two degrees, make probable?

It would make death probable.

Q. In what case would there be prospects of restoration?

If the fall be not more than four-tenths of a degree below normal?

Q. What is, generally speaking, more dangerous, the fall or rise from the normal point?

One degree below normal is more indication of a bad condition than two and a half degrees above the normal.

Q. In what does the danger consist in the first case?

In the degree of depression, then in continuance, then in descending progression.

Q. What does the slowly increasing low temperature generally do?

It will prepare the way to serious sickness or death.

Q. What else is striking, besides the variations of the temperature from the normal point?

The daily and hourly fluctuations.

Q. How much of a rise in temperature will a well-fed child show after a good meal?

A few tenths of a degree.

Q. How much will the temperature of a hungry child run up after taking nourishing food?

A full degree.

Q. If there is no rise of temperature during convalescence after eating, what does this prove?

That there is no nourishment secured from the food.

Q. What does it prove if there be a sudden or high rise above one degree?

That the food was too stimulating or heavy.

Q. What should always be effected of food during convalescence, to be beneficial?

It should increase the temperature a quarter to a half degree.

Q. When should this increase subside?

When digestion is over.

Pulse.

Q. Does the increase or decrease in the number of pulsations in a minute always prove a variation from the healthy pulse?

No.

Q. Which are qualities to notice in the pulse?

Frequency, regularity and fullness.

Q. How does a healthy pulse beat?

Steadily, evenly, from seventy to seventy-five times a minute.

Q. In what way are the number of pulsations affected by the position of the body?

They are more rapid in standing than in sitting down, and more in sitting than lying down.

Q. How may its regularity be interfered?

In two ways: the pulsations may be unequal in number and force, as few beats being from time to time more rapid and feeble than the rest, or intermitted altogether.

Q. By what is the fullness of the pulse determined?

By the sensation, the blood when passing through the artery, gives to the finger.

Q. When is the pulse said to be full?

If it strikes a large part of the finger pressing it.

Q. When small?

If it strikes a small part of the finger.

Q. When hard?

If in spite of firm pressure it forces its way under the finger.

Q. When soft?

When the pulsations scarcely cause a sensation to the finger.

Q. When is it said to be wiry?

When the pulsations are hard and small, the flow feeling like a wire.

Q. When jerking?

When the blood comes with hard, short knocks.

Q. When must all these different conditions be carefully considered?

When the pulse is examined as an indication of disease or health.

Q. What is extremely difficult to ascertain with young children?

The number of pulsations in a minute.

Q. What are, therefore, the things important to be noticed in examining the pulse of young children?

The regularity and fullness.

RESPIRATIONS.

Q. How often does a healthy adult breath?

Sixteen to eighteen times in a minute, without being conscious of the act of breathing.

Q. What must be noticed in sickness besides the variations from the healthy standard in number?

Whether the breathing is even and regular, or panting and short: whether it is from the upper or lower part of the chest.

Q. What must be noticed regarding pain?

Whether a deep, full inspiration can be taken without pain and if there is pain at what spot the pain is felt.

Q. What must be noticed about the position?

Whether the breathing is better in one position than in another, and in which it is the most distressing.

Q. What should be noticed about the sounds?

Whether the air makes any sounds as it passes through the lungs and air-passes and what kind of a sound.

Q. What about the difference in breathing?

Whether there be any difference between the breathing when sleeping and when awake and what it is.

URINE.

Q. What is drained away through the kidneys with the urine?

Many of the impurities of the blood and any excess of its watery ingredients.

Q. What is constantly shiftly?
The chemical composition of the urine.
Q. In what respect are there continual changes going on in the urine even with healthy persons?
In color and quantity daily passed.
Q. Which is the normal color of urine?
Like light amber or wheat straw.
Q. What is the daily normal quantity?
From thirty to fifty ounces?
Q. What is always the reaction in health?
Somewhat acid.
Q. What is the effect upon blue litmus paper?
It will turn red.
Q. When is it most acid?
Just before eating, especially before breakfast.
Q. When is it less acid?
During the process of digestion.
Q. How does it vary with age?
In children the quantity in proportion to the weight of the body is nearly twice as great as with adults.
Q. How does urine vary with sex?
The quantity being somewhat more abundant with females than males?
Q. How with season?
Less being passed in warm, dry weather, than at other times.
Q. What is the reason for this?
Because the perspiration is generally more profuse and urea passes off by the skin.
Q. How does it vary with the time of the day?
It is more deeply colored in the morning, paler during the forenoon, and deeper again in the afternoon and evening.
Q. Does food and drink cause any difference?
Many vegetables, acid fruits, liquids, etc., increase the quantity and produce other changes.

Q. What else causes certain chemical changes in the urine?
Violent exercise.

Q. What effect has mental exertion, over-study or hysteria upon it?
It increases the quantity of urine passed.

Q. Is the variation for one or two days from the normal condition of importance?
No.

Q. When should attention be given to the matter?
If the variations be frequent and long continued and especially if accompanied by other symptoms.

Q. What should be carefully noticed and reported in the different illnesses?
Every variation from the healthy condition.

Q. What do they indicate?
The presence and progress of the disease.

Q. From what should a specimen for examination be taken?
Either from the total accumulation of twenty-four hours or from that passed before breakfast.

Q. What care must be taken in getting a specimen of urine for examination?
To have it free from all impurities.

Q. How much will generally be wanted?
From three, six or eight ounces.

Q. In what kind of bottles should the urine for examination be preserved?
In clean, clear bottles.

Q. How should these bottles be cleaned?
First with warm water, then with cold water, and from time to time be boiled.

Q. How should the corks be?
Either new or washed and scraped.

Q. What must be attached to the bottle?
A label with the name of the patient, number of the room, the date and hour at which the urine was passed.

Q. What more must the nurse be able to tell?
What was eaten and what was the mental condition of the patient, whether any pain was felt or difficulty in passing urine.

Q. When must the urine be examined?
The same day it was passed.

Q. For what reason?
If it stands longer it will decompose.

DISINFECTING AND CARE IN COMMUNICABLE DISEASES.

Q. What is in communicable diseases one of the greatest responsibilities of a nurse?

Q. The prevention of contagion.
What is considered the most common conductor of contagion?

The atmosphere, which is everywhere more or less laden with microbes, especially in the sick room.

Q. What are they?
They are the lowest form of animal life soaring in the air, which we inhale.

Q. Are they visible?
Only under the microscope.

Q. What are they capable of?
Of a very rapid multiplication.

Q. What do they convey?
The specific poison.

Q. How do they lay for awhile?
Dormant.

Q. What do they do under suitable conditions?
They develop and multiply.

Q. What do they then produce?
The original disease.

Q. Where are the conditions of development found in some cases?
Within the body.

Q. How can the disease be transmitted in such cases?
Directly from one person to another.
Q. What does the germ do in other cases?
It only originates in the body.
Q. What does it require before it becomes infectious?
That it be developed outside.
Q. Which are the latter class?
Typhoid, yellow fever, cholera, dysentery.
Q. Of what are the other diseases commonly recognized as infectious?
By direct transmission.
Q. What is required after the exposure to contagion?
Some time for development.
Q. How do we call the time during which the poison remains concealed?
The period of incubation.
Q. When does smallpox commence to be contagious?
Even during the period of incubation.
Q. When is the risk of infection the greatest in measles and whooping cough?
Early in the disease, even before the rash and whoop appear.
Q. When is infection most dangerous in scarlet fever?
During the third and fourth week when the skin is peeling.
Q. How far does the poison of typhus appear to exert its influence?
Only within a limited range.
Q. How must the contact with the patient be in order to cause infection?
Moderately close.
Q. But how may the germs of smallpox and scarletina be carried about?
Indefinitely.

Q. What name have we for diseases which attack many people at the same time?

Epidemic.

Q. What are disinfectants?

Substances that destroy or render inert the germs of communicable diseases.

Q. What is the best disinfectant?

The most important is abundant fresh air.

Q. What will destroy the activity of all known disease germs?

Boiling for one half-hour.

Q. What should be done when the disease is declared?

The patient should at once be insolated as entirely as possible.

Q. How many persons should be attendants?

Not more than two.

Q. What must they avoid?

All contact with others.

Q. What must be carried out of the room?

All unnecessary articles and things that cannot be washed.

Q. Where should spoons, cups, etc., be kept that are used for the patient?

Near the room and should be washed there.

Q. What must be especially disinfected in cases of typhoid fever and dysentery?

The excrements and vessels.

Q. What should be poured down the closet from time to time?

Some disinfectant.

Q. What should be done where there is nothing but an outside closet or privy?

Some liquid disinfectant must be used and shovelsful of chloride of lime thrown down now and then.

Q. What must be done after the disease is ended in order to render the room fit for occupancy and to prevent the spread of infection?

The room must be thoroughly disinfected.

Q. How can this be done?

Spread out all the bed clothes and also all other clothes, open all the drawers and doors of wardrobes, wash stands, etc., close the windows and shutters tight, stop up all the cracks, chimney and key hole tight, then it is ready for disinfecting.

Q. Where is the disinfectant then placed?

In the middle or in different places of the room.

Q. What is used for disinfecting?

Formaldehyde gas.

Q. How is it used?

Have the lamp in the middle of the room, or if more than one is used at different places, light them and close the door.

Q. What may be used besides this?

Either chloride of lime and sulphuric acid, sulphur candles or some other disinfectant.

Q. What must the sister do after she has started the disinfectant?

Immediately leave the room and close it tight.

Q. How long should it remain closed?

From twelve to twenty-four hours.

Q. What must then be done?

The windows and doors should then be opened wide and the room thoroughly ventilated for several hours.

Q. What will render the disinfecting gas more effective?

If the room can be filled with steam just before the disinfectants are placed in.

Q. What must be done after the room is thoroughly ventilated?

It must be cleaned.

Q. What will be necessary in some cases?
That the furniture, wall and everything in the room be washed off with a solution of bichloride water.

Surgical Nursing.

Q. What is the first requisite in surgical nursing?
Absolute cleanliness.

Q. What must be faultlessly clean?
(1). Everything used about the wounds, patient and the bed.
(2). The places where dressings, instruments, etc., are kept.
(3). Everything about the person and dress of the nurse.

Q. To whom does the care of these things belong?
To the sister.

Q. When must all instruments be cleaned and sterilized?
Before and after using them for dressing a wound.

Q. What should not be allowed if oil or vaseline is required?
To put the finger into the bottle; take out a little with a spatul or a piece of gauze.

Q. What must be done if any is left?
It must be thrown away?

Q. What may never be done with dressings taken from a wound?
They must never be carried around from one bed to another.

Q. What should be done with them?
They must be removed from the room at once.

Q. What should be done with dressings which have been next to the wound?
They should be burnt, not washed.

Q. What must be done with such as are to be washed?
They must be disinfected.

Q. What should be avoided in handling dressings?
To soil your own hands.

Q. In what should old dressings be carried away?
In a basin or pail.

Q. In what case should the fingers not be used?
If a forcep will do just as well.

Q. In what must the hands always be washed before going from one case to another?
In a disinfecting solution.

Q. What should a sister do if the skin on her hand is broken, before going near a wound?
She should protect them with bits of plaster or collodion.

Q. What may be the consequence of a slight scratch?
To get blood-poison.

Q. Upon what cannot too much importance be laid?
Upon the necessity of absolute cleanliness in every way.

Q. What is cleanliness in its broadest sense?
The best antiseptic.

Q. What is of the greatest importance?
To have the hands clean, especially finger-nails.

Q. Why?
Because organic matter will find a lodgment under them.

Q. Is this organic matter always dangerous?
Yes.

Q. What has it undoubtedly been often the source of?
Of many a case of blood-poisoning.

Q. What is important before beginning a surgical dressing?
To have everything on hand likely to be needed.

Q. What is awkward for the nurse and fatiguing for the patient?
When a nurse has to leave in the midst of the process, to find something that has been forgotten.

Q. What can a sister not always tell when the doctor dresses a wound the first time?

What he may just call for.

Q. But what must she always have ready?

The things she knows he will want.

Q. What should the sister certainly know after she has seen the dressing once?

How to prepare for it the next time.

Q. What will be wanted in every case?

A protector for the bed (rubber sheet or Kelley cushion), towels, scissors, pins and basins.

Q. How many basins must be ready?

At least three—one to hold the fluid for washing the wound (irrigator), one to receive the old dressings and one to hold under to catch the discharge.

Q. What kind of basins are most convenient to catch up the discharge?

Crescent shaped, as they fit closely to any part of the body.

Q. What should never be done with old dressings?

They should never be pulled off forcibly.

Q. What should be done if they stick to the wound?

They should be irrigated until wet enough to come off easily.

Q. How should adhesive plaster strips be removed?

By taking hold of both ends and pulling them toward the wound from both directions evenly.

Q. What may be well to apply before removing the plaster?

New strips between the old ones.

Q. What will this prevent?

The wound from being pulled open.

Q. What will remove the traces from plaster?

Alcohol, ether or turpentine.

Q. What must a sister do if she is obliged to leave a wound undressed?

Cover it with a guard.

Q. What may be used for this purpose?

A piece of gauze, dry or saturated in an antiseptic solution.

Q. What should be done with dressings before they are thrown into the waste pail?

The fluid must be drained off.

Q. What must be done before dressings are applied?

The wound should be washed with some antiseptic solution.

Q. How is this done?

The wound is irrigated but never rubbed until quite clean.

Q. What is seldom necessary?

To touch the wound.

Q. With what should the edges be dried?

With the safest lint.

Q. How are severe burns or extensive wounds best dressed?

Only one part at a time.

Q. What kind of dressings are the best?

Dry or absorbant dressings.

Q. For what reason?

Because moisture promotes the development of germs and this is absorbed by absorbent dressings.

Q. What is the purpose of antiseptic treatment?

The destruction of infectious germs or the prevention of their multiplication.

Q. Do antiseptics do this?

Yes; they hinder the development of the germs and arrest their decomposition.

Q. What is much used for washing wounds?

Freshly boiled water, cooled in covered vessels.

Q. How are dressings sterilized?
By heat.

Q. Are chemical disinfectants necessary to sterilize them thoroughly?
No.

Q. What is the most reliable disinfectant and germicide?
Bichloride of mercury or corrosive sublimate.

Q. What else may be used?
Carbolic acid.

Q. Is it necessary to give full directions for the different dressings?
No; because each doctor has his own method and new ones are coming in vogue from time to time.

Q. But with what has the nurse to be familiar?
With the two above named germicides.

Q. What should she understand well?
How to manipulate and prepare them for use.

Q. In what form is bichloride of mercury bought.
In a coarse white powder or in tablets.

Q. In what is it soluble?
In boiling water or alcohol.

Q. Of what strength is it commonly used?
Varying from 1-1000 parts to 1-1500.

Q. How can you prepare a solution of 1-1000?
By dissolving thirty grains of the powder in three and one-half pints of boiling water.

Q. What should be added if the solution is not used at once?
Thirty grains of common salt.

Q. Why should the salt be added?
Because otherwise the solution is likely to decompose.

Q. What is the strongest solution used in surgery?
A solution of 1-1000.

Q. Upon what have bichloride solutions a corrosive effect?
Upon metals.

Q. For what purpose can it therefore not be used?
For disinfecting instruments.

Q. By what are gauze bandages and other materials used for dressings rendered antiseptic?
By impregnation with bichloride after prescribed methods.

Q. How does carbolic acid come when pure?
In transparent crystals.

Q. What is the strongest solution commonly used?
One to twenty parts.

Q. How can carbolic acid be liquified?
By placing the bottle containing the crystals into hot water.

Q. How can you prepare a twenty per cent. solution?
By pouring out one ounce of the carbolic acid and adding nineteen ounces of boiling water.

Q. What must be done after they are poured together?
It must be shaken vigorously until they are thoroughly mixed.

Q. Where must all carbolized solutions and dressings be kept?
In air-tight receptacles.

Q. For what reason?
Because it easily evaporates and then loses its strength.

Q. Why must they both be handled with great care?
Because they are both powerful poisons.

Q. What symptoms may they sometimes produce?
Toxic symptoms.

Q. When should a nurse always be on the lookout for constitutional effects?
When any powerful drug is used as an antiseptic.

Q. What should be carefully observed when carbolic acid is employed?
The urine.

Q. What is one of the earliest symptoms of this poisoning?

A dark green color of the urine.

Q. What materials are most frequently used for surgical dressings?

Plain, sterilized gauze, iodoform, bi-chloride or carbolized gauze, absorbent cotton, cotton wool, lint, etc.

Q. What sutures are used for bringing the edges of a wound together, holding them in place?

Silk, silver wire, cat gut or silk worm gut.

Q. What is used for tying arteries?

Ligatures of heavier silk or cat gut.

Q. How are these sutures and ligatures prepared?

In various methods.

Q. Are sponges used frequently for operations?

No; they are seldom used?

Q. In case they are used, how must they be treated?

They must be thoroughly cleaned and made aseptic.

Q. What is used instead of sponges?

Sponges made of cotton and gauze and sterilized, or pieces of aseptic gauze.

Q. Is the care of sponges, dressing materials and instruments used for operations, an important part of a surgeon's nurse?

Yes: it is very important.

Q. What else should she make herself acquainted with?

With the names of the instruments.

Q. Why?

So she can hand them without hesitation when called for by the operator.

Q. What is she expected to do after an operation?

To clean the instruments and return them to their cases.

Q. How must this be done?

Thoroughly, so that they are aseptically clean.

13—

Q. How must they be washed?

Carefully, because they are expensive and many of them so delicate that they will be ruined by careless handling.

Q. How should instruments with cutting edges be washed?

They must be taken by themselves and washed one by one.

Q. Should they ever be thrown in a heap together?

Never, but singly laid down. so that they will touch nothing to blunt their fine edges.

Q. What should be done with all instruments as far as practicable?

They should be disjointed, catches unlocked and tubes syringed.

Q. What should be washed off the instruments with soap and water before they are put in any disinfectant?

The blood.

Q. What must be removed?

Every stain.

Q. How should rough surfaces be cleaned?

They should be scrubbed with a brush.

Q. How can instruments, entirely of metal, be disinfected?

By sterilizing them ten to fifteen minutes.

Q. What instruments may not be put into hot water?

Those having ivory or bone handles.

Q. Why?

Because it would be likely to crack them.

Q. How can they be disinfected after they are washed?

They may be laid to soak in 1-20 carbolic solution.

Q. What must be done before they are laid away?

They must be perfectly dry.

Wounds.

Q. What is an incised wound?
A simple smooth cut like that of a knife.

Q. In what proportion is it dangerous?
In proportion to its depth.

Q. How is a wound called if the edges are torn?
A lacerated wound.

Q. Which is more painful, a lacerated cut or a sharp incision of the same extent?
A lacerated one.

Q. What can be more easily controlled in a lacerated wound?
A hemorrhage.

Q. What is a crush or bruise?
A laceration under the skin (subcutaneous).

Q. By what is a crush or bruised wound generally made?
By a blunt instrument.

Q. What will set up around the dead parts if the tissues are injured beyond recovery?
Ulceration.

Q. What will ulceration do in a wound?
It will separate the tissues.

Q. As what is this ulceration known?
As sloughing.

Q. How are gun-shot wounds called?
Crushed or tubular wounds.

Q. Are they painful?
Yes, they are very painful.

Q. By what are they likely to be accompanied?
By deep-seated inflammation.

Q. What are punctured wounds?
Those made by a sharp-pointed instrument.

Q. In what proportion are burns dangerous?
Not so much in proportion to their depth as to the extent of surface they involve.

Q. In what will a burn, covering half the surface of the body, result?

In death, from shock.

Q. Is there any prospects of recovery if so much as one-third of the surface is burned?

Yes.

Q. What is sometimes in great danger in severe burns?

The vitality of the part.

Q. What will often be the consequence in such cases?

The gangrenous part will slough off gradually with free formation of pus.

Q. How does such a wound heal?

Slowly by granulation.

Q. What are similar in effects to burns?

Scalds and frost-bites.

Q. How many degrees are there of frost-bites?

Two.

Q. What appearance have the frost-bitten parts if the vitality is merely suspended?

White, stiff and numb.

Q. What tendency do they develop upon return of circulation?

An inflammatory.

Q. Does vitality remain in the second degree?

No, it is completely destroyed.

Q. What supervenes upon thawing?

Gangrene.

Q. How many modes are there by which a wound of the soft tissues may heal?

Two.

Q. What is the first?

When two cleanly cut surfaces brought into close contact simply grow together.

Q. What is the second?

Granulation.

Q. By what may the healing of the granulating surfaces be hastened?

By skin-grafting.

Q. In what does this consist?

In placing upon it small portions of skin freshly cut from some parts of the patient or some other individual body.

Q. What precautions must be taken in grafting?

Antiseptic. The place where the skin is taken from must be antiseptically prepared.

Q. What is an abscess?

It is an accumulation of pus in any of the tissues or organs.

Q. What are drainage tubes used for?

To keep wounds open until they heal from the bottom and to carry off the pus.

Q. What are drainage tubes mostly made of?

Of rubber or glass, with holes in the sides, so that the pus may flow in from every direction.

Q. What may be used for the same purpose?

Strips of iodoform gauze and antiseptically prepared horse hair.

Q. What is pus?

Healthy pus is a thick, cream-colored, opaque discharge, smooth and insoluble in water.

Q. By what is the formation of pus accompanied?

By pain and throbbing.

Q. By what is it accompanied if extensive?

By fever and sometimes chills.

Q. How does it affect the system?

It is a steady drain.

Q. What must a patient suffering from a suppurating wound therefore have?

The most nourishing food to keep up his strength.

Q. In what does the treatment of wounds consist?
(1). In checking the hemorrhage.
(2). In removing foreign matters.
(3). In bringing separated surfaces into apposition.
(4). In excluding the air by some antiseptic dressing.

Q. Is it allowed to put two bad cases with suppurating wounds together into adjoining beds in a ward?

No, if it can be avoided.

Operations.

Q. How should the patient be prepared the day before the operation?

By giving a full bath and a physic the evening before.

Q. How should the part which is to be operated on be prepared?

It should be shaved, then washed thoroughly with a brush and green soap, rinsed with sterilized water.

Q. How can all the soap be removed?

By washing the part with alcohol.

Q. What must the sister do after she has washed the part with alcohol?

Wash her own hands in soap and water, and then in an antiseptic solution.

Q. How is the part to be operated on then prepared?

A bichloride dressing is then applied, or a green soap poultice, and held in place with a bandage.

Q. May the patient to be operated on eat a full supper the evening before?

No, only a light supper.

Q. What should be given on the morning of the operation?

A thorough enema.

Q. How long before the etherization must the patient fast entirely?

At least three hours.

Q. What, as a rule, is given to the patient about five or six hours before the operation?

A large cup of beef tea.

Q. What may be given one half hour before the operation?

A dose of brandy or whisky or one-fourth of a grain of morphine hypodermically.

Q. What must the patient do before going to the operating room?

Pass the urine.

Q. How should the hair be arranged?

Well combed and braided tightly.

Q. What must be taken out and what must be loosened?

Artificial teeth must be taken out and tight clothes and bands loosened.

Q. What clothes should be put on the patient?

A clean chemise, night-gown and stockings.

Q. How should the clothing be arranged?

So that they will be out of the way, well protected and easy to change if necessary.

Q. Where is the patient taken when ready for operation?

Into the anæsthetizing room.

Q. What is put on the patient there?

A pair of sterilized, cotton-flannel stockings, reaching up to the thighs.

Q. What is used for anæsthetizing?

Ether, chloroform, or a mixture of the two.

Q. How is ether administered?

Pour two or three drams at a time on an inhaler made large enough to fit over nose and mouth.

Q. Why must this inhaler be so large?

So as to exclude all the air.

Q. What will prevent irritation to that part of the face which is covered by the cone?

Anointing it with vaseline.

Q. How is chloroform given?

A few drops are sprinkled on a handkerchief or a small cone and held at a distance of two or three inches from the face.

Q. What must be avoided?

Touching the patient's face with the cone.

Q. For what reason?

Because a mixture of atmospheric air is needed.

Q. In what way is chloroform a better anæsthetic than ether.

It is more agreeable, rapid and less likely to nauseate

Q. In what way is it more dangerous?

It has a powerful depressing effect upon the heart.

Q. In what position must the patient be kept while under the influence of an anæsthetic?

Flat and the head low.

Q. Which are the signs of danger?

A feeble pulse, a livid face or extreme pallor, irregular and gasping respirations.

Q. Is the sister who is charged with giving the anæsthetic, allowed to divide her attention to anything else at the time?

No.

Q. Why?

Because the patient before her requires her undivided attention.

Q. Where should she keep her finger and her eyes?

The finger on the pulse and the eyes on the face of the patient.

Q. What should she do at the first warning indication?

Stop giving the vapor.

Q. Under whose direction and in whose presence should anæsthetic be given?

Always under the directions and in the presence of the doctor.

Q. Where is the patient taken after he is anæsthetized?

Into the operating room and placed on the operating table.

Q. What has the sister to do there?

After having prepared herself for assistance at an operation, she removes the dresssngs and surrounds the operating field with sterilized or bi-chloride towels.

Q. What must be placed over the operating field?

After it is washed again, a piece of sterilized or bi-chloride gauze is placed over it until the operator is ready.

Q. How is the operating room prepared?

It must be antiseptically clean, well ventilated and warmed.

Q. With what should everything therein be washed off?

With a bi-chloride solution.

Q. What must be done with basins, dressings, towels, etc., used at the operation, and the clothes of those assisting at the operation?

They must be sterilized.

Q. How long are clothes and dressings to be sterilized in steam?

Forty-five minutes.

Q. Where are dressings, sutures and other articles placed which will be needed at the operation?

On the dressing table.

Q. How should the sister prepare herself for assisting at an operation?

First, wash her hands thoroughly with brush and soap for five minutes, then trim the finger-nails to the quick.

Q. What will she then put on?

A white sterilized overdress and also a white veil.

Q. What is to be done next with her hands?

They are again washed with brush and soap for five minutes, then with alcohol or sterilized water two to three minutes.

Q. What must she do last?

Immerse the hands in bi-chloride solution for two minutes.

Q. Are the hands always prepared with these solutions?

No; if the operator wishes another method, it must be followed.

Q. After having washed her hands, is the sister allowed to touch anything not sterilized?

No.

Q. How many nurses generally assist at operations?

Three or four.

Q. How many handle the instruments?

Only one.

Q. What will the others do?

One gives the anæsthetic, the other gets and hands what may be needed and called for.

Q. What must the sister especially guard at operations?

Her eyes, avoiding everything that she is not obliged to see and by all means preserve her dignity and modesty.

Q. What is done after the operation?

The wound is dressed and bandages applied.

Q. On what is the patient then placed?

On the wheel-stretcher and taken back to bed.

Q. How must the bed be prepared?

Everything must be perfectly fresh and clean.

Q. What may be used in place of a pillow?

A towel.

Q. What should be placed in the bed some time before the patient returns?

Several hot water bottles, well protected and covered.

Q. Why should they be well covered?

They may cause serious burns while the patient is under the anæsthetic.

Q. What will check the nausea somewhat?

By applying a compress saturated with vinegar near the mouth and nostrils, so the patient will inhale the vinegar vapor.

Q. How should the patient be kept?

Warm and as quiet as possible, and free from all excitement.

Q. What must be allowed under no circumstances?

To sit up for any purpose.

Q. How should the wound made by the operation be arranged?

So that the dressing can be observed without waking the patient.

Q. When must this be especially watched closely?

During the first twenty-four hours.

Q. For what reason?

There may be a secondary hemorrhage.

Q. With what must the patient's strength be kept up?

With nourishing food in liquid form.

Q. How long must the liquid nourishment be kept up?

Until the doctor permits solid food.

Q. What occurs frequently after an operation or injury?

A shock.

Q. What is a shock?

A complete prostration of the nervous system.

Q. Which are the symptoms of a shock?

The patient becomes faint, and pale or trembling, the mind confused.

Q. With what is the surface covered?

With perspiration.

Q. By what other symptoms is a shock often accompanied?

By nausea and involuntary passages.

Q. How may a shock easily result?

Fatally.

Q. What will favor a shock?
Loss of blood or debility.

Q. What may be given to the patient?
Brandy and beef tea.

Q. How should it be given if the patient cannot swallow?
By enema.

Q. What should be applied to the extremities?
Heat, but with all precautions mentioned above.

Q. What is especially valuable in such cases?
Hypodermic medication.

Q. What will prove a powerful stimulant?
A hot water bag over the heart, but great precaution must be used.

Q. What is the patient never allowed to do?
To make any effort to get up or exert himself.

Q. What is the third great danger to which the patient is liable after a surgical operation?
Blood poisoning (pyaemia).

Q. What is the most contagious form of pyaemia?
Erysipelas.

Q. What must be done if any patient developes symptoms of it?
He must be promptly insolated.

Q. In what wounds is it most frequent?
In lacerated wounds and in those of the head and hands.

Q. How do the edges become?
Red and swollen.

Q. How is the temperature and pulse?
The temperature is high, the pulse quick.

Q. By what other symptoms is it accompanied?
By headache, nausea and coated tongue.

Q. In how many days may the disease terminate favorably?
In ten to fourteen days, but it is often fatal?

Q. By what is pyaemia usually initiated?
With a chill, accompanied by high temperature.
Q. By what is this temperature followed?
By profuse perspiration.
Q. How is the pulse and how is the expression of the face?
The pulse is fast and feeble, the expression of the face anxious.
Q. Where are abscesses liable to form?
In parts of the body distant from the wound, especially in the joints.
Q. At what intervals may the chill recur?
From eight to twenty-four hours.
Q. In how many days is this disease usually fatal?
From four to twelve days.
Q. What must by all means be maintained?
The strength of the patient and the fever kept down.
Q. What is of the utmost importance?
Free ventilation and utmost cleanliness.
Q. What is a rather less dangerous form of blood poisoning than the former?
Scepticaema.
Q. Does it occur with repeated chills?
No.
Q. By what is it characterized?
By a high but more regular fever and a general typhoid condition.
Q. What is usually a fatal complication with wounds?
Tetanous.
Q. What wounds does it generally follow?
Slight wounds oftener than severe wounds.
Q. From what does it often result?
From exposure of the wound to cold.
Q. By what is it marked?
By a certain muscular rigidity.
Q. How does this rigidity set in?
Very abruptly.

Q. With what does it begin?
With the muscles of the throat and jaw?
Q. How and how long does it extend?
It extends gradually until the whole body is in continuous convulsions.
Q. What is important in these cases?
That the symptoms be recognized early and reported to the doctor.

LAPORATOMY.

Q. How long should a patient who is to be operated for laporatomy or abdominal section be at the hospital before the operation?
At least three or four days.
Q. How must the patient be prepared for the operation?
The evening or the day preceding the operation the patient is given a special bath, the abdomen is shaved and a soap poultice applied, which is kept in place with a roller bandage.
Q. What is sometimes preferred to the soap poultice?
A bichloride dressing.
Q. How long is this left on?
All night.
Q. What is done in the morning?
A thorough enema is given and a specimen of urine saved for examination.
Q. What is then removed?
If a soap poultice has been applied, that is removed, the abdomen is then first thoroughly scrubbed and washed with alcohol.
Q. What is then applied?
A towel or piece of gauze soaked in 1-1000 bichloride solution and wrung out fairly dry is now laid on the abdomen and secured with a bandage.
Q. When is this removed?
Not until the last moment before the operation.

Q. What is laid on the abdomen when the bichloride dressing is removed?

Four sterilized towels, one on each side, one at the top and one at the bottom, leaving a space in the center for the incision.

Q. How are the corners fastened together?

With sterilized safety pins.

Q. What is placed over the center until the surgeon is ready to make the incision?

A piece of bichloride gauze.

Q. At what degree is the operating room to be generally heated for laporatomy?

Eighty degrees.

Q. How should the sister enter the operating room?

With surgically clean hands, apron and veil.

Q. When the doctor is ready what will be the duty of the sister?

To wait on the doctor, to keep out of the way and to see that nothing is handed to the doctor which has touched any doubtful surface.

Q. What must the sister do if she rests her hands on the table or touches anything that is not sterilized?

She must wash her hands again and merely dip them in an antiseptic solution.

Q. What must be done if anything should chance to fall on the floor?

It must be laid aside and on no account be used again.

Q. When the operation is going on what should a sister always remember?

That she is present as an assistant, not as a spectator.

Q. What must she therefore look out for?

To see what is wanted next and not exactly what the surgeon is doing.

Q. What must be done after the operation is completed?

The dressings are to be applied.

Q. How must these dressings be?

Aseptic beyond suspicion.

Q. What is done after the dressings are applied?

The patient is put to bed.

Q. What must now be ready for the patient?

Hot water bottles well protected and stimulants.

Q. Why is generally the shock in laporatomy so great?

On account of the number of nerve-centers involved.

Q. When may the pillow be placed under the patient's head?

Not until the effects of the anæsthetic have worn off.

Q. How should the abdomen be supported if there is any vomiting?

It should be supported by a hand on each side of the wound.

Q. What will this avoid?

This will avoid any strain upon the sutures.

Q. What is very important to distinguish in this case?

The ether-vomiting after laparotomy from the vomiting of early developing of peritonitis.

Q. How does the vomiting occur if caused by ether?

Everything is rejected as soon as swallowed, and it stops only when the stomach is empty.

Q. How may it be in acute peritonitis?

The patient may take nourishment for hours and then suddenly throw up a large quantity of greenish or yellowish fluid, having a sour smell.

Q. In what time does peritonitis usually develop?

In twelve to forty eight hours after the operation.

Q. What will frequently control the ether-vomiting if it is persistent?

The application of ice-cold cloths to the throat.

Q. Should the patient be allowed to overload her stomach with ice water?

No, water must be withheld as much as possible.

Q. What will allay the thirst better than ice water?

Very hot water.

Q. Of what other advantage is hot water in this case?

It will not leave the mouth so parch as ice water, nor is there any danger that the patient will desire to drink too much of it.

Q. What is very necessary during the first twenty-four hours?

To watch for any symptoms of hemorrhage.

Q. What should the nurse do if she suspects a hemorrhage?

She should remove the pillow, elevate the foot end of the bed slightly, apply hot water bottles to the extremities, and notify the surgeon at once.

Q. How often should the urine be drawn?

Unless otherwise instructed, every six hours for the first forty-eight hours.

Q. What must be done with the urine?

It must be measured, carefully observed and a specimen saved for examination.

Q. What is important to note about the bowels?

Whether the bowels have moved or not, and the character of the defecations.

Q. What is one of the possible complications to be looked out for in this case?

Paralysis of the intestines, but this only the doctor can decide.

Q. Is it important that the clinical record be kept full and accurate in these cases?

Yes.

Q. How often should the temperature, pulse and respirations be taken and marked?

Every four hours, the first few days.

Q. What nourishment should be given?

Always in liquid form, as is ordered by the surgeon.

Q. What nourishment and medication may be necessary?

Rectal, which should be administered with the greatest care.

Q. How may tympanites be relieved?

By the introduction of a tube into the rectum through which the gas may escape.

Q. How must the patient be turned on her side after permission is given by the doctor to do it?

The whole body is turned at once so gently that no strain or twist will come upon the wound.

Q. What must be observed when the time has come for the stitches to be removed?

The same antiseptic precautions as when they were put in.

Q. If the patient is not taken out of bed, with what should the bed be protected?

With a rubber sheet or a Kelly cushion.

Q. What must be spread over these?

Towels wrung out in bi-chloride 1-1000.

RULES FOR SISTERS IN THE SURGICAL WARD AND OPERATING ROOM.

1. Sisters should wear clean cotton or linen overdress with sleeves at the time of operation and when the surgeon is making his rounds.

2. Sisters having charge of surgical cases, should have the fingernails carefully trimmed down to the quick, and they should use the nailbrush with soap for five minutes before each operation. They should not do any work which would cause the hands to chap; first, because the dirt gets into chapped places and cannot be easily removed; secondly, they might get poison in the chaps and blood-poison would be the consequence.

3. After the hands are washed, they should not be used about the nose, mouth, or put into the pocket.

4. During the operation the hands should touch nothing that has not been sterilized.

5. A sister who handles the body of a patient, or gives the anæsthetic, or who carries water or removes slops, should not touch the instruments or dressings.

6. Instruments which have dropped on the floor or elsewhere should not be used in the same operation again.

7. Bandages, instruments and dressings of all kinds should be sterilized before every operation. Pans and dishes and instruments should be scrubbed with sapolio after each operation and steamed.

8. All patients for abdominal operations should have a thorough warm bath the evening before.

9. One sister only should handle the instruments, gauze and thread, and she should do nothing else during the operation.

10. The ordinary scissors should not be used for cutting gauze and thread; only scissors which have been prepared for it should be used.

11. Solution for use in the steamer or sterilizer: Carbonate of soda, one-half dram to one quart of water.

Gynæcological Cases.

Q. How are disorders of the female reproductive organism classified?

As gynæcological.

Q. What is the first important thing for a nurse to understand in case a patient is to be examined?

The method of physical examination of the pelvic organs and what assistance the physician may require of her.

Q: What will be required of the nurse for a mere digital examination?

Very little besides her presence and to wait upon the doctor as he may desire.

Q. What is the sister never allowed to do at such an examination?

To leave the patient alone with the doctor.

Q. How should a patient be prepared for the examination?

If possible, she should have a bath, a vaginal douche and the external parts must be clean.

Q. In what position may a patient be placed for an instrumental examination?

Either in a dorsal, knee-chest or lateral position.

Q. How must the patient lie in a dorsal position?

Flat on her back, with the knees elevated.

Q. How in the knee-chest position?

Just the reverse, the hips elevated.

Q. On what does the weight then rest?

On the knees.

Q. What should lie flat against the table?

The chest, and should be supported by the elbows.

Q. As what is the third and most common position known?

As Sims position.

Q. On what side is the patient placed in this position?

On the left side, with the left buttock on the extreme left corner of the table, the left arm behind her, and the knees drawn up, the right above the left.

Q. Where do the head and right arm of the patient come?

To the right side of the table.

Q. From what must the patient be protected?

From unnecessary exposure.

Q. How should the limbs be protected?

A light blanket or sheet should be placed lengthwise, so that each leg is covered separate.

Q. What should a sister do if she places the patient in a dorsal position?

She must raise the patient's knees herself.

Q. What will she avoid by this?

Any strain on the part of the patient.

Q. Should the patient ever be allowed to rise from her position without first turning to the side?

Never, because the strain is too great.

Q. How is the speculum prepared for use?

By first dipping it for an instant into hot water to warm it, then oiling the outer surface.

Q. If the Sims speculum is used, who must hold it in its place?

The sister, if required.

Q. Where must she stand?

Behind the patient, facing the operator.

Q. How should she stand?

Firm on both feet, in a position that she can maintain steadily for a long time if necessary.

Q. Where may she rest her right arm?

On the right hip to steady it.

Q. What hand retains the speculum?

The right hand.

Q. In what position must it be held?

In the same position in which it is handed.

Q. What other instruments are needed for these cases?

Depressor, sound, probe, tenaculum, curette, uterine dressing, forceps, applicator, cotton holders, dilators and pessaries.

Q. What are more commonly employed in the treatment of uterine cases?

Various tampons and other local dressings.

Q. How is the ordinary tampon made?

By cutting a strip of absorbent cotton about three inches wide and rolling it up, not too tightly, until it has a diameter of about an inch and a half.

Q. Where is the twine or stout thread tied?

About the middle of the roll, leaving ends of about six inches hanging.

Q. For what are these ends left?

For convenience in removal.

Q. For what purpose are they used?

They are used to keep the parts in proper position and to apply medication.

Q. How is the butterfly tampon made?

Take a thin, flat piece of cotton with a string tied about the middle.

Q. How is a kitetail tampon made?

It is a series of bunches of cotton tied at intervals of two or three inches along one string.

Q. By what other means is vaginal medication applied?

By means of suppositories and douches.

Q. What is used for a douche?

It is either medicated or of pure water, as directed.

Q. At what temperature are hot douches usually ordered?

At a temperature of 112 to 118 degrees Fahr.

Q. How are they given?

They are usually ordered as prolonged douches, from two to four quarts given.

Q. How should the patient lie?

The patient should lie on her back, with the hips elevated until they are several inches higher than the shoulders.

Q. Why is it absolutely necessary to have the patient in this position?

Because a douche taken standing or sitting is of very little use.

Q. What is put under the patient?

A douche pan.

Q. What syringe is used?

A fountain syringe, as it has a steady flow under low pressure.

Q. How should it be held or hung?

At a considerable height to give good force to the flow.

Q. What kind of a nozzle should be used?

A long nozzle which has three or four openings, and it must be introduced well before the water is injected.

Q. What care must be taken when giving a hot douche?

That the mucous membrane is not blistered by the hot tube.

Q. What tubes are preferable to metal ones?

Ivory or hard rubber.

Q. What tubes and nozzles are mostly used?

Glass tubes, because they can be made and kept perfectly aseptic.

Q. How can this be done?

By first boiling them and keeping them in an antiseptic solution or a piece of sterilized gauze.

Q. Which are the most common gynæcological operations?

Those for laceration of the cervix and perinæum.

Q. What must be carefully noted and reported in the preparation of the patient?

The previous condition of the bowels and the character of any vaginal discharge.

Q. How should the patient be prepared?

The patient should have a full bath the day before and, if necessary, the parts shaved.

Q. May the sister shave the parts?

No; this should be done by the doctor or whoever may be appointed by him.

Q. What should be given in the evening?

A purgative, and in the morning an enema, if possible six hours before the operation, so the rectum may become empty and quiet.

Q. What besides this must be given in the morning?

An antiseptic douche.

Q. About what should the nurse obtain definite directions from the surgeon after an operation of the cervix?

About emptying the bladder.

Q. What should be done after an operation of the perineum?

Tie the patient's knees together, that no unconscious movement on her part may bring a strain upon the stitches.

Q. What might be the consequence if there be much strain upon the stitches?

The desirable result will be hindered, even if the stitches are not torn out.

Q. Of what does the treatment consist?

Of rest and keeping up absolute cleanliness.

Q. Upon whom does the failure or success of an operation largely depend?

Upon the nurse.

Q. What may a little careless manipulation on her part do?

It may render useless the best skill of the operator.

Q. What must be done if the patient is allowed to pass urine voluntarily?

The sutured parts must be gently irrigated each time.

Q. What care must be taken if the patient is catherized?

That no drops of urine fall upon the wound.

Q. How can this be avoided?

By placing a piece of absorbent cotton between it and the catheter.

Q. What must the nurse do after and during defecation?

See that there is no strain upon the sutures.

Q. What must be exercised in all manipulation in such cases?

The utmost gentleness.

Q. How long must the most scrupulous cleanliness be kept up?

Until the stitches are removed, which is about the ninth day.

FRACTURES.

Q. What are the most common injuries of bones?
Fractures.

Q. What is a simple fracture?
It is a fracture in which the bone is only divided.

Q. What is the fracture called if there is a wound of the soft parts so that the broken bone communicates with the outer air?
A compound fracture.

Q. Does every flesh wound, existing together with a fracture, render it a compound fracture?
No, only then, when it leads to the seat of the fracture.

Q. What is it called if the bone is broken in two or more places?
A multiple fracture.

Q. What is it called if the bone is broken into several small fragments?
A communicated fracture.

Q. What is it called if some joint or cavity are involved in the injury?
A complicated fracture.

Q. What is it called when one end of the broken bone is driven forcibly into the other?
An impacted fracture.

Q. When is a fracture serious?
When there is a great injury of the tissues, or when a joint is involved.

Q. What are signs of a fracture?
Pain, distortion, loss of function or unnatural movement or crepitus.

Q. What is crepitus?
It is the grating made by rubbing together the ends of the broken bone.

Q. By what is a fracture of the spine indicated?

By loss of sensation and power of motion below the point of injury.

Q. What will a patient complain of with a fractured rib?

Of sharp pain when he takes a deep breath or coughs, and will often spit blood.

Q. What is the danger from a fractured rib?

It is of injury to the heart, lungs or large blood-vessels.

Q. In what does the treatment of fracture consist?

In putting the fragments into proper position by the doctor and keeping them there until they have united.

Q. What may be used for this purpose?

Splints made of wood, tin, paste-board, leather, felt or anything that will hold the bone accurately and firmly in place.

Q. What must be done with the splint before it is applied?

It must be well padded.

Q. What are frequently used in place of splints?

Bandages, saturated with glue, starch or plaster of paris.

Q. What is usually preferred for a compound fracture?

A fracture box.

Q. How should this be prepared?

It must be padded well.

Q. What will then answer the purpose of the splints?

The sides of the box to which the limb is bandaged.

Q. What must be done with the limb before any apparatus is applied?

It must be carefully washed and dried.

Q. What must be dusted over it to absorb perspiration?

Fine starch or toilet powder.

Q. What is frequently applied in fractures of the thigh?

An extension weight.

Q. Where is this attached?
It is attached to the foot with adhesive straps.
Q. How should a broken limb be lifted?
The parts both above and below the point of fracture must be lifted.
Q. What care must be taken?
Neither to shorten nor to twist the limb.
Q. What may be the consequence of unskillful handling?
A single fracture may be converted into a compound one.
Q. What is dislocation?
It is the displacement of one of the bony structures of a joint from the other.
Q. What is a sprain?
It is the laceration or stretching of the ligaments with twisting of the joint.

HEMORRHAGE.

Q. What is a hemorrhage?
The escape of blood from its containing vessels.
Q. How may it be described?
As arterial, venous or capillary hemorrhage.
Q. Of what color is the blood from an artery?
Bright red.
Q. How will it spurt out?
In jets of considerable force from the side of the wound nearest to the heart.
Q. Of what color is venous blood?
It is of a dark purplish hue.
Q. How does it move?
In a sluggish, continuous flow, mainly on the side farthest from the heart.
Q. What is a capillary hemorrhage?
A mere oozing of blood.
Q. Which of the three is the most dangerous?
The first.

Q. If a hemorrhage is not checked promptly, how may it prove in many cases?

Fatal.

Q. How is a hemorrhage, following short after an operation, named?

A secondary hemorrhage.

Q. How long is there any danger of a hemorrhage after an operation?

The first twenty-four hours, but it is by no means over until the wound is well healed.

Q. What favors the formation of clots and the arterial contraction?

The application of heat or cold.

Q. What will reduce the force with which the blood is sent to the artery?

Elevating the injured part.

Q. What must be done if blood is spurting from an artery?

Pressure must be applied.

Q. How can this be done?

With the finger, by pressing upon the bleeding point or the vessels which supply it.

Q. What may be done if the bleeding vessel is too deep to be reached by the finger?

The wound can be plugged with gauze.

Q. How can this be done most effectively?

Cut a number of small bits, each a little larger, beginning with the smallest, press them well into the wound.

Q. How far should the pile extend?

To some height about the surrounding level.

Q. By what may it be secured?

By a tight bandage.

Q. Where can such compression be made successfully?

Only over a bony surface.

Q. In what cases does it become difficult and sometimes even impossible to control the hemorrhage?

If the artery is imbedded in the muscles.

Q. How are wounds of the head and face apt to bleed?

Profusely.

Q. How can this bleeding be almost always controlled?

By direct pressure, as the skull affords firm counter-pressure.

Q. What may be applied, in case the pressure of the finger cannot be made forcible enough, or if the pressure cannot be kept up long?

A tourniquet.

Q. What should be done with the limb before the tourniquet is applied?

It should be elevated as high as possible.

Q. What may be used in the absence of the regular apparatus?

A handkerchief or a piece of muslin with a hard knot or a smooth stone tied in the middle.

Q. How should this be fastened around the limb?

Rather loose and twisted with a stick.

Q. Where must the knot be kept?

Over the injured artery until pressure enough is made to completely occlude it.

Q. How long may a tourniquet remain on the arm?

One hour.

Q. How long on the thigh?

For two hours, no longer.

Q. For what reason?

As the part will die if its nutrition is cut off too long.

Q. What may be used if the artery cannot be reached with a tourniquet?

The handle of a long key, or a blunt stick, suitably covered, may be forcibly pressed against it.

Q. What is often used to prevent hemorrhage during an operation upon the limb?

A very tight rubber bandage spirally from its extremity to a point above the site of the proposed incision.

Q. What should be around the place where this stops?

A piece of rubber tubing with hooks at the end to be fastened.

Q. What is to be removed when the circulation will be found almost completely cut off?

The rubber bandage.

Q. What should be kept on hand where there is danger of secondary hemorrhage?

A piece of heavy rubber tubing, which may be used in place of a tourniquet.

Q. What will sometimes aid in arresting a hemorrhage?

Flexion of a limb.

Q. How is this done?

Put in the joint a firm roll of lint, against which pressure will come when the joint is bent.

Q. What may the patient be directed to do in case of bleeding from the palm of the hand?

To clasp closely a wad of lint.

Q. How should he hold the hand at the same time?

High above the head.

Q. What other means are there for arresting a hemorrhage?

Application of medicines externally, such as perchloride of iron, alum, gallic acid.

Q. With what is obstinate bleeding from a small point sometimes checked?

By touching it with caustic.

Q. What may be employed by the surgeon when the bleeding is from many vessels over a large surface?

A cautery.

Q. What is a cautery?

The application of a hot iron.

Q. When is the cautery or external medicine used?
Only then when no other means will answer.
Q. What method is most commonly used to arrest hemorrhage of the artery?
Ligation.
Q. How is this done?
The artery is picked up with a pair of forceps and a ligature tied firmly around it.
Q. What ligatures were formerly used for this purpose?
Ligatures of strong, soft silk.
Q. What ligatures are employed now in wounds which are to be completely closed?
Cat-gut ligatures, because they absorb and do not need to be removed.
Q. Which is the most dangerous form of venous hemorrhage?
That from rupture or a varicose vein.
Q. Where should pressure, heat or cold be applied in such a case?
Below the bleeding point, the limb being elevated.
Q. Why is pressure made below the point of bleeding?
Because above the point it would be useless and absurd.
Q. Why is ligation avoided?
Because it is likely to cause inflammation of the vein.
Q. What should be worn in cases where there is danger of such a rupture?
An elastic stocking or bandage.
Q. When should this be put on?
Before getting up in the morning.
Q. Is cappilary hemorrhage dangerous?
No, it can easily be checked by cold, by position or by hot, not merely by warm water.
Q. How must the hot water be used?
As hot as it can be borne.

Q. Why will warm water not do?

Because it will increase the flow of blood.

Q. How does the blood come up if it comes from the lungs?

It is coughed up, is bright red and more or less frothy.

Q. From where does blood, supposed to come from the lungs, frequently come?

From the mouth or throat.

Q. What is this called?

Hæmotysis.

Q. What is the vomiting of blood called?

Hæmatemesis.

Q. What is the patient likely to have before it occurs?

A sense of fullness and oppression.

Q. How does the blood come up?

A large quantity of dark blood, mixed with food, is thrown up without much nausea.

Q. How should the patient be kept in both cases?

Quiet and cool, the head elevated.

Q. What may be given to the patient?

Bits of ice, which should be swallowed whole, if possible.

Q. What may be applied externally?

Ice-cold cloths.

Q. What kind of food may be given?

Only fluid food, cold, in small quantities.

Q. What may be done when an exhausting hemorrhage has occurred, after its source has been controlled?

The limbs may be tightly bandaged from their extremities to the trunk.

Q. For what purpose?

To prevent the circulation of blood which is needed by the vital organs.

Q. What care must be taken?

Not to leave them on too long.

Q. What often appears in the stool after the vomiting of blood?

Some blood, as a dark, tarry substance.

Q. What may be given for a hemorrhage from the bowels?

Ice-cold injections or other medicated solutions as ordered.

Q. What should be applied over the abdomen?

Cold applications.

Q. What is sometimes ordered internally?

Small doses of opium.

Q. In what cases may it occur?

In the course of typhoid or yellow fever.

Q. What is most commonly the cause of such a hemorrhage?

Hemorrhoids.

Q. How must the patient be kept in this case?

Quiet and lying down.

Q. From where does blood in the urine come?

From the kidneys, bladder or urethea.

Q. What must be noted?

Whether it appears at the beginning or at the end of the micturiation, and whether the passage is accompanied by pain or not.

Q. How is the blood from the kidneys?

Dark and clotted.

Q. How is it from the bladder?

Generally clear.

Q. What is generally ordered in cases of uterine hemorrhage, especially when following an operation?

A vaginal douche of hot water; or hot solution of alum.

Q. What is given internally?

Fluid extract of ergot or gallic acid.

Q. What other local hemorrhage needs special attention?

Epistaxis (bleeding from the nose).

15—

Q. What is often the cause of it?
An accident or a spontaneous outbreak.

Q. If spontaneous, as what may it be looked upon?
As an effort of nature to relieve the head.

Q. But if this is too severe, how can it be checked?
By pressing the facial artery at the root of the nose.

Q. Where should cold applications be applied?
To the forehead and back of the neck.

Q. What position should never be taken?
Leaning over a basin.

Q. How should you make the patient stand?
Erect, throw his head back and elevate his arms while you hold a cold, damp sponge to the nostrils.

Q. What is done if the bleeding still persists?
The nostrils are syringed with salt and water, ice-cold, one dram to one pint, or with a solution of alum or iron.

Q. What must the patient avoid?
Blowing the nose.

Q. What is necessary if all other means fail?
That the surgeon plug the nose.

Q. Why is this process resorted to when all others have proved ineffectual?
Because it is very painful.

EMERGENCIES.

Q. What above all things should a sister show in case of any accident?
Coolness and presence of mind, no hurry, no confusion whatever.

Q. What is often the consequence of any severe injury?
A complete prostration of the vital powers.

Q. How is this called?
A shock.

Q. How does the patient appear in this state?
Sometimes conscious, the surface of the body pale and covered with cold perspiration.

Q. What is the temperature?
Abnormal.
Q. How is the pulse?
Feeble.
Q. How are the nostrils?
Dilated.
Q. How are the eye-lids?
Drooping.
Q. What other symptoms may be observed?
Mental and muscular weakness.
Q. What may happen in less severe cases?
Nausea and vomiting.
Q. How should the head be kept?
Low.
Q. What should be given to the patient?
Stimulants until the heart's action is revived.
Q. To what parts should heat be applied?
To the extremities and the pit of the stomach.
Q. What is the best stimulant when there is nausea?
Brandy.
Q. What is to be done if the patient cannot swallow?
Inject brandy or camphorated oil hypodermically.
Q. What manifests many of the same signs as a shock?
Fainting or syncope.
Q. By what is this unconsciousness in fainting occasioned?
By insufficient supply of blood to the brain.
Q. What must never be done with the head?
It must never be raised, but kept as low or even lower than the feet.
Q. What is next important for the patient?
Plenty of fresh air.
Q. What may be given by inhalation?
Ammonia, but not too strong.

Fractures and Dislocations.

Q. What should be done in case of fracture of the limb if it cannot be set at once.

Temporary splints, made of paste-board, shingles, etc., may be applied until the surgeon arrives.

Q. How can it be bandaged if no splint is at hand?

To a straight, padded stick, or even to the other leg.

Q. What should be applied in fracture of the knee-cap bone (patela)?

The foot should be elevated to a considerable height and the leg kept straight by a long splint at the back.

Q. What should be put under the knee?

A pad.

Q. What should be applied for fractured ribs?

Keep the patient quiet in bed, put a broad bandage tightly around the chest.

Q. What should be noted particularly?

Whether there is any blood raised.

Q. How should the patient be kept if skull fracture is suspected?

In a quiet, dark room, on his back, with head slightly raised and cold cloths be applied to head.

Q. What should be done for fracture of the jaw?

The mouth should be closed and fixed in place with a bandage.

Q. Where do sprains frequently occur?

At the wrist and ankle.

Q. How can they be treated?

They may be soaked in hot water and bandaged with hot cloths.

Q. What may be used on a painful crushed finger or toe?

It may be wrapped in soft cloths wet with hot water and a little laudanum.

Q. About what must special care be taken with contused and lacerated wounds?

The cleaning out of blood clots.

Q. In what cases is rest especially important?

With all extensive wounds, especially those of the thoric and abdominal cavities.

Q. How should the patient be laid when the chest is injured?

Lay the patient rather on the wounded side than on the other.

Q. What is important with a punctured wound?

To keep it open until it heals from the bottom.

Q. What should be done if this puncture be made by splinter or thorn?

The splinter must be entirely removed, not by poking at it, but by making a sharp incision along its course.

Q. What should be done if the splinter goes under the fingernail?

Trim or split the fingernail down to the end of the splinter.

Q. What should be done in case of the bite of a venomous snake or other probably poisoned wound?

The bleeding should be rather encouraged than checked.

Q. How can this be done?

The limb should be tied tight if possible above the point of injury at once, the wound should be sucked or cupping glasses applied?

Q. What else may be applied?

Ammonia water.

Q. What may be done if possible?

The wound may be cauterized.

Q. What may always be regarded as suspicious?

The bite of any animal.

Q. What bite is said to be more dangerous than that of a dog?

The bite of a rat or cat.

Q. How should stings of insects be treated?

With cool lotions.

Q. With what may the eruption caused by poisoning be treated?

With a saturated solution of carbonate of soda.

Q. What are generally the most alarming accidents that will happen from time to time?

Those caused by fire.

Q. What should be done if your own clothes catch on fire?

Lie down and roll and keep your mouth closed.

Q. What should be done if you see another person in the same danger?

Throw the person down and wrap a shawl, rug or any heavy woolen thing at hand to extinguish the flames.

Q. Where should you begin to wrap?

At the head, keeping the flames as much as possible from the face.

Q. What is always the great danger in case of fire accident?

That of inhaling the flames.

Q. What is the first object in the treatment of burns and scalds?

To exclude the air.

Q. What will this at once allay?

The pain.

Q. What can be done if the injury is only on the surface?

Sprinkle it thickly with carbonate of soda and tie a wet bandage over it until the pain subsides.

Q. How may the part then be protected from the action of the air?

By painting it over with the white of an egg.

Q. What is even a better application?

Flexible collodian.

Q. What other plan can be used for relief?

Dust the surface with flour and cover with a thick layer of cotton wool.

Q. If the burn is severe enough to have blistered or destroyed the outer skin (cuticle) what is generally used?

Carron oil, with equal parts of linseed oil and lime water.

Q. What is even better?

Pure olive oil or vaseline.

Q. By what is a severe burn usually accompanied?

By a shock.

Q. How are burns produced by strong acids treated?

The same as those by fire.

Q. What may make a severe burn?

Lime or caustic.

Q. How may these be treated?

With a solution of diluted vinegar or lemon juice, about a teaspoonful to a cup of water.

Q. What should be done if fragments of lime get into the eye?

Bathe it with a solution of vinegar or lemon without wasting time in trying to pick it out.

Q. How may dust or cinders be cleared out of the eye?

By drawing the upper lid well down over the lower one and at the same time blowing the nose forcibly.

Q. What can be done if a particle gets caught in the lower lid?

Draw down the lower lid by the lashes, direct the patient to turn the eye-ball toward the nose.

Q. With what can any foreign body then be wiped out of the eye?

With a soft handkerchief.

Q. What can be done if it is under the upper lid?

This can be turned up over a knitting needle or a small pencil and then wiped out.

Q. In what direction should the eye always be rubbed?

Always towards the nose.

Q. What should be done if an insect gets into the ear?

The sufferer should be laid on the other side, the tube of the ear be straightened by pulling the tip upward and slightly backward.

Q. With what should the ear then be filled?

With olive oil or glycerine; then the insect will float on the surface.

Q. What should be done if there be a hard substance in the ear?

Hold the ear downward and syringe gently with warm water.

Q. What special care must be taken in this case?

Not to close the opening of the ear with the syringe.

Q. In what cases should this never be done?

If it is anything that will swell by moisture, as a bean or pea.

Q. Is it advisable to poke at such substances?

Never, for it may be driven beyond reach.

Q. Who should be sent for?

The doctor, as soon as possible.

Q. What should be done if there is any foreign body in the nostril?

Make the patient take a full breath, then close the mouth and other nostril firmly, when the air, having no other way to escape, may expel the obstruction.

Q. What should be done, if this fails, and the object is in sight?

Compress the nostril above it to prevent its being pushed up farther, and hook it out with a hair-pin or bent wire.

Q. What should be done if anything is stuck in the throat or oesophagus?

It can be hooked out the same way, if it is too far down to be reached with the finger?

Q. In what case is it advisable to push the object down?

Only in case it were digestible substance.

Q. What may be taken to carry the obstruction down?

A piece of bread may be swallowed.

Q. By what is a foreign body generally expelled out of the windpipe?

By coughing.

Q. What part is very sensitive?

The trachea.

Q. What will sometimes be of use if the person is choking?

A blow on the back.

Q. What can be done if it is a child?

It can be taken up by the feet and held head down, while several blows can be given between the shoulders.

Q. What may be done if a person is apparently drowned?

Before beginning artificial respiration, turn the face down for a moment and clean out with the finger the mucous that may be at the base of the tongue.

Q. In what other cases must this be done?

In cases of strangulation.

Q. What must be removed from the neck?

Everything tight.

Q. From where must a patient be kept suffering from severe cold?

From the heat, otherwise there is danger of sloughing of the frost bitten parts.

Q. Where should a person be taken who is found frozen?

He should be taken to a cold room, undressed, rubbed with snow or wrapped in cloths wrung out in ice water.

Q. How long should the friction be continued, especially about the extremities?

Until circulation seems restored.

Q. What may be resorted to if the natural respiration is at a standstill?

Artificial respiration.

Q. What should be given as soon as the patient is able to swallow?

Brandy or beeftea.

Q. How should he be brought into the warmer air?
Only by degrees.

Q. In what case is the same plan pursued?
With any frost bitten parts.

Q. What should the aim be?
To restore vitality without inducing sloughing.

Q. Will a person always feel it if parts of the body are frozen?
Parts of the body may be frozen without the sufferer's knowledge, as numbness precedes the latter stages of freezing.

Q. What should not be done with a tendency to chillblains?
Cold feet should not be too quickly heated.

Q. How should the feet be kept?
Always warm and loosely clad.

Q. What will relieve the itching?
Painting them with iodine will relieve the itching.

Q. What may develope if neglected?
Painful and intractable ulcers.

Q. Where does a hernia of the peritonaeum with prostration of the abdominal contents take place?
Either in the groin or lower part of the abdomen.

Q. What does the tumor often contain?
A loop of small intestines.

Q. Which are the symptoms?
Intense pain, obstinate constipation and persistent vomiting.

Q. What should be done in such cases?
Put an ice bag over the swelling, give no food, no physic, very little drink, and send for the surgeon at once.

Q. What should be done in cases where a patient is found insensible?
The head should be kept cool and get medical advice as soon as possible.

Q. What should be done if poison is taken into the stomach?

The stomach is to be evacuated by emetics.

Q. What makes an excellent emetic?

Warm water and salt, or ground mustard, a tablespoonful mixed in a cup of water and given repeatedly.

Q. What will sometimes produce vomiting?

Tickling in the back of the throat with the finger or a feather.

Q. How should emetics be given?

Half a pint to a pint at the time.

Q. What should be given after some irritant poison?

Some bland fluid to soothe irritated parts.

Q. What may be given?

The white of an egg, milk, flour and water, gruel, olive or castor oil.

The Human Body.

Q. How is the human body divided?

Into head, trunk and limbs.

Q. Of what does the head consist?

Of the arched skull, and this is covered with the scalp.

Q. What is on the front of the skull?

The forhead.

Q. What is below the forehead?

Two cavities with the eyes.

Q. What is between the eyes?

The nose, with the nostrils adjusted to the nasal bone.

Q. What is on both sides of the nose?

The cheeks, which cover the upper jaw bone.

Q. How far do the cheeks extend?

They extend without interruption to the low jaw bone.

Q. What is in the middle of the face below the nose?

The mouth, with upper and lower lip; lower down is the chin.

Q. What are situated on both sides of the head?

The ear trumpets, which collect and carry the sounds to the internal ear.

Q. Through what is the head united to the trunk?

Through the neck.

Q. What is found in the back of the neck?

The spinal column.

Q. What is situated in the front of the throat?

Commencing from the spinal column, past the gullet (œsophagus), farther on in front of the trachea or wind-pipe, with the larynx.

Q. What does the larynx contain?

The vocal cords.

Q. What is found on both sides of the throat?

Large veins, which lead and bring back blood from the brain, and also important nerves.

Q. How many sides has the trunk of the human body?

The front and the back.

Q. What is situated in front of the shoulder-blade on both sides of the throat?

The collar-bone (clavicle).

Q. How far does it extend?

From the upper corner of the breast-bone to the shoulder-blade.

Q. What forms the upper part of the trunk?

The thorax.

Q. What is placed in the chest on both sides?

The lungs.

Q. What is situated on the left side near the middle line?

The heart.

Q. What is found at the lower end of the chest in the center?

The pit of the stomach.

Q. What is noticed on the back of the trunk at the top?
Two flat, three-cornered bones, which almost meet in the center, the shoulder-blades (scapula).

Q. What follows lower down?
The ribs, attached to both sides of the spinal column.

Q. Where are the upper joints connected with the trunk?
In the shoulder.

Q. Of what do the upper limbs consist?
The upper arm, the lower arm, hands and fingers.

Q. What is the space called between the chest and arm, there where the arm is joined to the shoulder?
The arm-pit (axilla).

Q. Of what do the lower limbs consist?
Of the thigh, leg and foot.

Q. Where are the lower limbs connected to the trunk?
In the hip.

Q. What are the bones?
They are the frame-work of the body.

Q. What do they constitute when joined as in a living man?
The skeleton.

Bones of the Head.

Q. How are the bones of the head divided?
Into the bones of the head and the bones of the face.

Q. How many bones are in the head?
Eight.

Q. How are they joined together in a grown person?
By close-fitting tight seams which present an appearance along their edges like the teeth of a saw.

Q. What is inclosed in the cavity of the skull?
The brain with its membranes.

Q. Are the bones connected firmly in the skulls of children?
No; they are joined together by membraneous connections.

Q. What is felt through the skin there, where two or three bones meet?

Soft, impressible places, called fontanelles.

Q. Where can one of them be distinctly felt?

On the top of the head somewhat further than the forehead (the anterior fontanelle).

Q. How long can this be felt?

Frequently up to the second year.

Q. How many bones form the frame of the lower part of the head—the face?

Fourteen.

Q. Which is the most moveable bone in the face?

The lower jaw bone, which moves in two joints just below the skull.

Q. What is found in the upper lower jaw bone?

The teeth.

Q. How many teeth has a grown person?

Thirty-two in all—sixteen above and sixteen below.

BONES OF THE TRUNK.

Q. How many bones form the trunk?

Fifty-seven.

Q. Of what do they consist?

Of the spinal column or backbone, the thorax and basin or pelvis.

Q. Of what does the spinal column consist?

It is built out of single round bones which have projections?

Q. What are these single bones called?

Vertebrae.

Q. What is found in the middle of these round bones built upon each other or vertebræ?

The spinal canal, and in them the spinal marrow or spinal cord.

Q. Where is the spinal column joined to the head?

At the base of the skull.

Q. On what does the lower part of the spinal column rest?

On the small of the back or sacrum.

Q. How are these vertebræ divided?

There are seven cervical vertebræ, twelve dorsal vertebræ and five lumbar vertebræ.

Q. What forms the thorax?

The ribs and breastbone with the backbone.

Q. How is it formed?

The ribs—twelve on each side—are joined to the backbone: they come around like an arch and are connected in front to the breastbone.

Q. How many ribs are joined to the breastbone or sternum?

The seven upper ones.

Q. What are they called?

The true ribs.

Q. What are the lower ribs called?

The short or false ribs.

Q. What are the two lowest ribs called?

The floating ribs.

Q. What is the thorax?

It is the second large cavity containing the lungs and heart.

Q. What forms the basin or pelvis?

The lower lumbar vertebræ, the small of the back or sacrum and the hip.

Q. What is found on the outer side of the hip bone?

A socket into which the head of the thigh bone (or famur) fits.

Q. What do the above mentioned bones form with their membraneous and soft parts?

The third large cavity, which contains the stomach, the intestines, the liver, the spleen, the kidneys and bladder.

Bones of the Upper Limbs.

Q. What is situated on the upper end of the back?

A flat, three-cornered bone, called shoulder-blade (or scapula).

Q. What rests upon this bone?

The collar-bone (clavicle).

Q. To where does the collar-bone extend?

To the upper corner of the breast-bone (or sternum).

Q. What is situated at one corner of the shoulder-blade?

A hollow with a smooth surface, into which the head of the upper arm-bones are placed.

Q. What kind of a bone is the upper arm-bone, or so-called humerus?

It is a long, strong, round bone.

Q. What has it at its lower end?

A kind of a roll, which is joined to the two bones of the fore-arm.

Q. How many bones has the fore-arm?

Two—one on the side of the thumb and the other on the side of the little finger.

Q. How is the bone on the side of the thumb called?

The radius.

Q. How the one on the side of the little finger?

The ulna.

Q. With what are the two bones joined movable together?

With ligaments.

Q. To what are they joined at the lower end?

To the wrist.

Q. How is the hand divided?

Into the wrist (or carpus), palm (metacarpus) and fingers (or phalanges).

Q. What forms the wrist?

Eight short irregular bones.

Q. How are they joined together?

By ligaments, into a compact bunch.

Q. What forms the palm of the hand?
Five long tube-shaped bones (metacarpal bones).
Q. How many bones has the fore-finger?
Three (called phalanges).
Q. How many the thumb?
Two.

Bones of the Lower Limbs.

Q. How is the lower limb divided?
Into hip, thigh and foot.
Q. What is the part called between the knee and hip?
The thigh.
Q. What is the part called from the knee to the foot?
The leg.
Q. How are the lower limbs joined to the trunk?
By the head of the thigh-bone (femur), which fits into a socket of the hip-bone.
Q. Which is the longest and strongest bone in the human body?
The thigh-bone (femur).
Q. What is found at its lower end?
A broad, round surface for the knee-joint.
Q. To what is the surface of the thigh-bone (or femur) joined?
To the strongest bone of the leg, the shin (tibia).
Q. What does this connection form?
The knee-joint.
Q. What is in front of the knee-joint?
A small, three-cornered bone, with round edges, called the knee-pan, knee-cap (or patella).
Q. With what is the knee-pan (or patella) joined to the thigh and leg?
With ligaments.
Q. How many bones has the leg?
It has two, the shin-bone (or tibia) and the fibula.

Q. What kind of a bone is the shin-bone (tibia)?
It is strong, three-cornered, tube-shaped bone.

Q. Where is it situated?
At the innerside, on the side of the big toe, and is the principal bearer of the body while walking and standing.

Q. What kind of a bone is the fibula?
A long, slender bone on the outer side of the leg and much weaker than the shin-bone.

Q. Where is it joined to the shin-bone?
Above and below.

Q. To what are both bones joined at the lower end?
To the ankle-bone of the foot.

Q. Of what does the foot consist?
Of the tarsus or middle foot, or metatarsus, the toes or phalanges.

Q. How many bones are in the tarsus?
Seven irregular bones.

Q. What do they form?
The ankle, the heel and instep.

Q. What do the middle foot or metatarsal bones form?
The flat of the foot and part of the instep.

Q. How many are in each foot?
Five.

Q. What are joined to these five bones?
Fourteen phalanges, forming the toes.

Q. How is the foot shaped?
It is arched and elastic.

Q. Where does the weight rest?
On the heel and ball of the toes.

SKIN.

Q. With what is the human body covered?
With a soft, smooth but strong covering called skin.

Q. How many layers has the skin?
Two.

Q. What is the top layer called?
The epidermis or cuticle.
Q. What is the deep layer of the skin called?
The true skin or derma.
Q. What is imbedded in the true skin?
The sweat glands and sebatious glands.
Q. Where do they end?
On the surface of the top skin.
Q. Of what does the top skin or epidermis consist?
Of a thin, almost transparent, layer.
Q. What does this top layer do constantly?
It scales off and is renewed as it wears off.
Q. What grows on some parts of the body from the chin?
Hair; the roots of them lie deep in the skin.
Q. What grows from the skin besides the hair?
The nails on fingers and toes.
Q. What do the sebatious glands manufacture?
They manufacture an oily fluid.

MUSCLES.

Q. What are muscles commonly called?
Flesh.
Q. What are muscles?
Dark red masses gathered up in bundles.
Q. Where are the muscles situated?
They are arranged over the skeleton, most of them being attached to a bone at each end.
Q. What ability do they possess?
The ability to expand and contract.
Q. Is this ability alike in all muscles?
No; in some it is greater than others, according to their size and use.
Q. How are all the muscles of a limb arranged in a living body?
They are bound together and covered with a fibrous tissue.

Q. Through what are the muscles commonly attached to the bone?

By means of tendons.

Q. What are tendons?

Glistening cords of fibrous tissue.

Q. How many muscles are in the body?

More than five hundred.

BRAIN.

Q. Where is the brain found?

It fills the chief cavity of the skull.

Q. What color has it?

It is a grayish, white mass.

Q. Is it only one mass?

No; there are several masses joined together.

Q. How is it divided?

Into the large brain (cerebrum) and small brain (cerebellum).

Q. Where is the large brain or the cerebrum placed?

It is placed in the cavity of the skull from the forehead to the back of the head.

Q. Where is the smaller brain?

It is in the back of the head, low down.

Q. Of what service is the brain?

It is the organ employed to think, feel and will.

Q. What is a continuation of both, the cerebrum and cerebellum?

The spinal cord which occupies the spinal canal in the backbone.

Q. How thick and how long is this cord?

It is about half an inch thick and eighteen inches long.

Q. What originates from the brain and spinal cord?

Small white-yellowish strings—the nerves.

Q. To where do they extend?

They go out of the spinal canal through openings between the vertebræ, and extend to all parts of the body.

Q. What is connected by them?

The different parts of the body are connected with the brain spinal cord.

Q. To what may the nervous system be compared?

To the telegraphic system of a railroad.

Q. What place do the nerves take?

They are the wires which take and carry messages from the brain and spinal cord to the most exterior parts of the body.

Q. What has each muscle?

Each muscle has its nerve which gives it the power to move, to contract or relax.

Q. What is the consequence, if the nerves of feeling are cut off from a certain part of the body?

It will no longer obey your will; will not move; is lame.

Q. What will the sensory nerves do?

They carry messages from the outside or the deep parts of the body to the brain.

Q. What is the consequence if the sensory nerves are cut off from the brain?

That part is without feeling; feels no pain; no warmth: no cold; no pressure.

Q. What does a third kind of nerves rule?

They rule the unwilled actions, called reflex actions, such as heart action, digestion, respiration.

The Organs of Sense.

Q. What rules the organs of sense?

A special group of nerves.

Q. With what do we smell?

With the nerves of smell.

Q. Where do they spread?

In the top of the nasal cavities.

Q. With what do we taste?

With nerves of taste, which spread on the top of the tongue and the roof of the mouth.

Q. By what are external sounds perceived, such as noise, etc.?

By the nerve of hearing.

Q. Where are external sounds carried to?

To the ear-drum.

Q. To where is it carried from the ear-drum?

To a chain of small, fine bones, the nerves of hearing, and then to the brain.

Q. With what do we see and distinguish light from dark?

With the nerves of sight or optic nerve.

Q. Where are these nerves?

In the eye.

Q. How are the eyes shaped?

They have an oval form and are constructed out of several membranes.

Q. Where are the eyes situated?

In the cavities of the skull, called orbits.

Q. What is the middle of the eye?

The pupil.

The Lungs.

Q. Where are the lungs?

They are in the chest and occupy almost entirely this cavity

Q. What are the lungs?

They are soft masses of little cells with very thin walls.

Q. With what are the lungs covered?

With the pleurae.

Q. What is the pleurae?

Two air-tight sacs, one for each lung, one layer covers the lung and the other lines the chest wall.

Q. To what are the lungs first connected?

To the bronchial tubes, higher up with the trachea, then with the larynx, with mouth and nose, and by these with outside air.

Q. For what purpose do the lungs serve?

For breathing.

Q. How is it done?

By the expansion and contraction of the chest and the descending and the ascending of the diaphragm.

Q. What may this be called?

Inspiration and expiration.

Q. What is inhaled with the act of inspiration?

Air, which is a material substance, composed of gases and acid.

Q. What comes in contact with this air in the lungs?

The dark red blood which circulates in various veins in the lungs.

Q. What effect has this upon the blood?

It is purified, gets a bright red color and is rendered fit for circulation and sustaining of the body.

Q. What is thrown off from the blood by expiration?

Carbonic acid gas.

Q. What is the consequence of this?

That in a room where there are many persons and no renewal takes place, the air becomes close and injurious.

The Heart.

Q. What is the heart?

It is a muscular mass which contains several cavities and is about as large as a fist.

Q. As what is it characterized?

As a hollow muscle.

Q. How is it shaped?

Like a pear, with the small end pointing down, and to the left.

Q. How is the interior of the heart divided?

Into four cavities. The upper cavities are called auricles, the lower ones ventricles.

Q. What enter into each auricle?

Large veins, which bring blood back from the body.

Q. What is found between the auricle and ventricle?

A valve, which consists of three thin flaps.

Q. What does this prevent?

It prevents the blood from passing back from the ventricle into the auricle.

Q. From where does the blood flow out of the right ventricle?

Into the large pulmonary artery, which soon divides into two branches and extends into both lungs.

Q. What opens out of the left ventricle?

The great artery of the body, the aorta, which gives off numerous branches, which go to all parts of the body.

Blood Vessels.

Q. With what are all arteries and veins connected?

With the heart.

Q. What are blood vessels?

They are pipes which serve for the circulation of the blood.

Q. What are the blood vessels called?

Veins, which carry dark red blood, and arteries which carry bright red blood.

Q. What are connected to the arteries and veins?

Numerous small blood vessels, called capillaries.

Q. What is formed by the capillaries?

The connection between arteries and veins.

The Most Important Arteries.

Q. What arteries carry the blood to the head?

The carotid arteries; they pass up on each side of the neck.

Q. What arteries lie behind the collar-bone?
The sub-clavian.
Q. How far does it extend?
To arm-pit, and is called axillary artery.
Q. To where does it then go?
To the elbow, and is called brachial.
Q. What does it do at the elbow?
It is divided into the radial and ulnar; the radial lies at the thumb side of the fore-arm and is the one in which the pulse is commonly felt.
Q. What is the artery called which carries the main stream to the thigh?
The femoral artery; it proceeds from the groin to the knee close along the bone.
Q. What is it called in the leg?
The tibial artery; lower down it divides into several branches leading to the foot.

Veins.

Q. Where do arteries extend to at last?
Into the small blood vessels or capillaries?
Q. What takes its beginning in these capillaries?
The veins, which bring the blood back from the extremities into always larger vessels and finally to the heart.
Q. Where do the veins run?
Generally along side of the arteries.
Q. Where does the venous blood come together finally?
In two large veins, which empty themselves into the right auricle.

Blood.

Q. What is blood?
It is a red fluid, not transparent, having a salty taste.
Q. Of what does blood consist?
Of blood corpuscles, watery substance called plasma, and a coagulative substance.

Circulation of the Blood in the Body.

Q. What does the heart do?
It moves constantly from the first moment of life until death.

Q. Where is its beat felt?
On the left side of the chest.

Q. What causes the beating?
The extension and contraction of the auricles and ventricles.

Q. What is forced out by this movement?
The blood contained in the cavities, so as to make room for another supply.

Q. To where is the blood forced from the left ventricle?
Into the large artery called aorta.

Q. To where is it led from this?
Into always smaller branches to the most distant parts of the body.

Q. How is the blood brought back to the heart?
After it flows from the capillaries of the arteries into the capillaries of the veins, then always into larger veins, which finally bring it back to the heart.

Q. Into where do the veins empty the blood?
Into the right auricle.

Q. Where is it forced to from here?
Into the right ventricle.

Q. What is caused by the contraction of the right auricle?
The blood is forced through the pulmary artery into the lungs.

Q. What is done in the lungs?
The blood is purified and becomes bright-red again.

Q. To where does it return then?
To the left ventricle and commences its circulation again.

DIGESTION.

Q. In what does digestion take place?

In the alimentary canal.

Q. Where does this commence?

In the mouth, and ends in the large intestine.

Q. With what is nourishment tasted after it is taken into the mouth?

With the tongue and palate.

Q. With what is it chewed?

With the teeth.

Q. With what is food mixed while chewing is going on?

With saliva, which is produced by the saliva glands in the mouth, and is thereby formed into a mass, so as to render it so that it can be swallowed.

Q. How does the food reach the stomach?

By passing from the mouth through the oesophagus.

Q. What is the stomach?

It is a membraneous sack situated on the left side of the trunk somewhat below the short ribs, and extends to the pit of the stomach.

Q. What does digestion mean?

The changes that take place in the food, as it passes through the alimentary canal, by which it is fitted to be taken up into the blood.

Q. What is connected with the stomach?

The intestines, first the small, then the large intestine.

Q. How long is the intestine?

About six times the length of the human body.

Q. With what is it lined?

With mucus membrane.

Q. What is connected with the small intestines?

The gall bladder, which furnishes bile needed for digestion.

Q. What is the liver?

It is a large organ or gland, situated at the lower border of the ribs on the right side?

Q. What does the liver make?

It makes the bile.

Q. What are the kidneys?

They are two organs situated on each side of the small of the back.

Q. What do they do?

They carry off waste and matters from the blood.

Q. What shape have they?

The shape of a bean.

Q. Where is the urine carried to from the kidneys?

Into the bladder.

www.ingramcontent.com/pod-product-compliance
Lightning Source LLC
Chambersburg PA
CBHW032107220426
43664CB00008B/1166